Trading Rules II

More Strategies for Success

William F. Eng

Dearborn
Financial Publishing, Inc.

Managing Editor: Jack L. Kiburz
Senior Associate Editor: Karen A. Christensen
Cover Design: Jill Shimabukuro
Interior Design: Lucy Jenkins

©1996 by William F. Eng

Published by Dearborn Financial Publishing, Inc.

Printed in the United States of America

96 97 98 10 9 8 7 6 5 4 3 2 1

Library of Congress Cataloging-in-Publication Data
Eng, William F.
  Trading rules II: more strategies for success / William F. Eng.
    p. cm.
  Includes index.
  ISBN 0-7931-1242-7 (cloth)
  1. Stocks.   2. Options (Finance)   3. Futures.   I. Title.
HG4521.E584   1995
332.64--dc20   95-34622
                                                                        CIP

CONTENTS

CONTENTS

PREFACE

In retrospect you and I have come a long way from the first opening pages of *Trading Rules: Strategies for Success*, which was published in 1990 and has sold many thousands of copies around the world.

In *Trading Rules*, I describe the 360-degree learning wheel theory, which breaks down a trader's career into three time periods or trips around the wheel of wisdom. You cannot acquire complete learning and knowledge in your first decade of trading. Nor can you achieve them in your second decade. Only after the third decade can you fully acquire knowledge of the markets; only at this point in your learning cycle as a trader can you really develop an understanding of what market action is all about.

Now, five years later, I've written another book which gives you an additional 50 trading rules that will help you explore and profit from market action even more. In *Trading Rules II* you will find ideas similar to those found in the original *Trading Rules*. You will also encounter new ideas and perspectives not found in any other book, such as one of the lesser known reasons why stocks split.

The goal of such information is to make you more market savvy so that you can determine when, what, and how you should trade the market. Remember: The correct application of the trading techniques is centered on determining the market cycle. A hammer can be used to hammer a nail, not a staple; a moving average technique can be used effectively to trade trending markets, not trading markets. Guiding you toward making the right trades for the cycle is the major, and very important, benefit of this book.

If your experience is similar to that of other readers, you'll find that the ideas and tactics in *Trading Rules* and *Trading Rules II* will improve your performance. In *Trading Rules,* I tell you about a friend who, after ten years of trading the markets, started to make money two years ago. Three years ago, he had still been working on his own overtrading problem. Two years ago, he made a 70 percent annual return. He closed out his trading accounts records for 1994 and came out a big winner, two years in a row. I asked him what his biggest loss was and he told me he lost $1500 on a soybean trade. Then I asked him what his biggest winner was and he told me over $15,000 on coffee. The loss to win profit was 1 to 10. He is a winner! It took him a long, long time to get to this point where he no longer overtrades and always, always uses stop loss orders. He thanked me for pointing out some of his flaws in trading.

As we ended our conversation he told me he was thinking of getting a part-time job selling life insurance. When I asked him why, he replied: "I get really bored trading the markets. I put on my positions after I figure out what I want to do. Then I just sit there and watch the market go in my favor. I sit at home watching my monitor for six hours a day. What can you suggest to kill my boredom?"

I laughed out loud and told him I, too, was still searching for a suitable answer to that question for myself. Writing books was one way for me to accomplish this.

In effect we are our own worst enemies when it comes to successful trading. By learning, practicing and using these trading rules, we can also become our own best allies.

William F. Eng
Chicago, IL

RULE 1

Learn To Be a Good Loser, but Keep Your Name in the Hat

Like a lottery where you have to buy one ticket to get even a chance to win, you must also have a position in the market before you can take advantage of an upward or downward move.

Over my years in the trading business in all its forms and functions, from the runner to the clerk, from bank trader to sole proprietor trader, I have learned a lot.

After experiencing the excitement of trading for my own account—shoving and pushing other traders in the pit, getting jabbed with sharpened pencils, screamed at by escapees from a bootcamp for tyro rock band trainees, stomped on by stampeding sellers after a two-point Fed funds interest-rate hike, mangled by flailing elbows and cracked knuckles, bruised and battered by panicked buyers after a two-point Fed funds interest-rate drop, and watching a trader collapse from a heart attack while the activity in the pit continued to swirl around him—I realized that youth in floor trading ends at the age of 32.

Well, after you've done anything for a long time, you might need a refreshing change. Steaks are great, but every so often you have a hankering for hamburgers. After years of trading for my own account, I decided to try another aspect of the business. So I became a broker to see what it was like.

Briefly for six months, I delved into the role of salesman, and I learned to become a closer. I was never good at generating any commissions for myself. My clients made money from my buy and sell recommendations, but I had to go back to trading for my own account to make ends meet. Clients would pay me $35 in gross commissions, and I would manage their positions to four-figure winners.

Keeping your name in the hat hit home during my stint as a broker. Several years ago, one of my clients was extremely bullish on D-Marks: He had read about the fundamentals pointing to the direction of the upward move in the D-Marks, his technical indicators showed a buy and he had enough money in the account to carry some big positions.

He concluded that he should take a position in his trading account. So he bought some D-Marks and waited.

He waited for one day, two days, three days, . . . up to one week. Nothing happened. In the second week, we both waited since I was beginning to get just as anxious as he was. Nothing happened in the second week, either. We discussed the scenario again, and each confirmed that the scenario was ripe for a bull market move.

But nothing happened. At the end of the third week, we lost our patience, and we were ready to take his hat out of the ring. In frustration my client gave me instructions to sell out his positions.

Just as I was sending orders to sell out his positions at the market, a thought occurred to me. The fundamentals pointed to a bullish move. The technicals indicated that the D-Marks should be bought. The problem was our timing. As a conscientious broker, how could I help my client out of that dilemma?

I looked at the open position. I looked at the stop loss orders we had entered at the time of the trades. I reasoned that my commissions on the trades would be paid to me anytime the trades were closed out. We could close them out today. We could close them out tomorrow. We literally could close them out at any time. So what was the hurry? I didn't need the commission.

I called up my client and told him the value of my commissions. He agreed. I told him that he was going to pay me the commission as soon as the trades were closed. He agreed with me on that also. Then I asked him, what was his rush to close out the trades and give me the commission?

No answer. After some thought, he agreed that I was right. His analysis pointed to a buy, and his actions made him long. However, his timing, as of this discussion, was off. I reasoned with him that we had stop orders in place. We knew exactly how much we could lose on the long positions. If the stop orders got caught, he would still pay me the commissions. What was the advantage of closing out the trades by forcing a sale at the market? It would have been close to scratch trades, so the loss to equity would have been minimal. Was there an advantage to closing out the trades, he asked me.

I told him, no, there wasn't an advantage to closing out the trades. We had already predetermined our loss potential with the stop orders, and we had figured out the commissions. So why not leave the trades as they were?

This was a simple solution to a timing miscue. With our stop orders in place, we proceeded to look at other trading opportunities. Four weeks from the inception of the trades, the D-Marks finally moved bullishly with a vengeance. The play lasted an additional two weeks. My client made money because he had positions in the market. If he had closed out the trades without market-dictated reasons, he would not have had any positions in the market. It was conceivable that when the bull move started in earnest, the client would not have been able to get in for whatever reason.

Here, the client had bought a lottery ticket. All he had to do was wait until the conditions were right for his scenario to unfold. If he hadn't kept his hat in the ring by staying with his open position, he wouldn't have made any money. To the extent that his analyses proved correct, he still had to wait for the market and its participants to recognize these facts.

You've got to play to win. If you are going to play, you've got to realize that you will have to pay the costs. One of the costs is that you always have to have a position in the market you are trading to make the money.

Oh, yes, my client made $72,000, and my net commissions were about $220. I failed as a broker, but my client made money! At times, I wished I had myself as a broker.

After putzing around for several more months, I had to go back to trading to pay my bills. Back to the same miserable floor trading environment. The trader recovered from his heart attack. The elbows weren't as sharp as I had remembered them to be. The jostling, pushing, and shoving were much milder, Fed funds moved only half a point at a crack, and everything seemed much friendlier.

RULE 2

Trade on Probabilities, but Guard Against the Possibilities

One of the major misconceptions is many people believe that we are particularly different from the rest of the group. We believe that we don't fall in the norm; we believe that we aren't a component of a statistic. Yet we are.

Practical rules are probabilities. If we follow state and federal laws, we probably won't have any legal problems. However, we must always be on guard for the exception to the rules. The exception will always get us into a lot of trouble especially when we are not prepared.

Years ago I went to an art opening for a one-man show of an artist whose works were spiraling upwards in market value. I took one look at the works and remarked to a friend that I could make the same kind of art. The recognized artist's works were montages made from clippings from newspapers and magazines. These were simple pieces that a child could easily duplicate.

Overhearing my comments, the artist pointed out, "Yes, you can duplicate these by yourself, but can you spend a lifetime doing these? What about the consistency and texture after you've created ten of these? Or how about after creating 100 of these miniature works?"

At first, I thought to myself, "Do a hundred pieces? That's crazy. Who would want to do these for a lifetime? I can find better things to do with my time. Better it be you than me to waste my life." I withheld these thoughts, however. Later, I reconsidered what the artist had said to me. The impact of what he told me has since affected my life as a trader.

I can make a trade now and then, hitting on some great plays every so often. So can you. You can monitor one market and jump right on board when it gets going. Getting home runs is easy in baseball if all you do is wait until the right pitch comes along; in trading the markets all I have to do is spend a year looking at one market and then position when the conditions are right. This, however, doesn't make me a professional trader. If anything, this exemplifies me as a dilettante, not an expert in the trading business.

What makes me a trader is *consistency*. This ability marks athletes as professionals. Their output and consistency of execution make writers and artists what they are.

All professionals base their careers on a set of norms in their respective areas. The market-defined norms are based on *probability*. These norms are not arbitrarily based on what *possibility* is. Once professionals have established a norm in their performance, they can then project out into possibility and grab for the golden ring. It is at these moments in history when they surprisingly shoot past the norm and break previously established records.

A good baseball player who has a consistent 0.280 runs batted in (RBI) every year for the past five years will probably continue to do so in the sixth year. This is his own "market defined probability." These numbers are not based arbitrarily on what "possibility" is. If, in the sixth year, our baseball player batted several deviations better, to about a 0.325 RBI average, the realm of "possibility" has entered into his probability statistics. The baseball player's agent would push for a new contract and want a hefty salary increase. The team's owner must, however, recognize that the sixth year's RBI statistic is the realization of a possibility phenomenon, not a probability statistic. The owner would be foolish to grant the new contract with a higher salary. The probability is that in the seventh year, the player's RBI statistic will return to a 0.280 RBI!

The probability is what takes them from a promising base, and the ever-so-often occurring possibility projects them far above the base. A higher and higher base will eventually make even the least possible a probability. If the baseball player continues to improve his game, his agent will eventually be able to persuade the owner to offer a new and better contract. Without the base upon which structure is developed, the probability that possibility can exist has diminished!

To get into the trading game you must learn to scalp. From scalping you learn to position trade. From position trading you learn how to play market moves for their maximum profits. In the meantime you are developing a set of norms for your performance, a base for your professional trading successes. Upon these successes your infrastructure is evolving slowly. A successful trader's career follows this natural progression.

You can make deviations from the norm, but they take up so much more time to balance out. The deviations are side excursions which will detract you from focusing on what is necessary for your success.

So, can you then argue that the deviations are not beneficial? To the contrary. If you have the resources, or in most cases, the need, to have created these deviations, then you must work them out and dispense with them.

Therefore, I cannot fault you for having created those deviations which will detract you from an expedient resolution to trading success. These are your burdens to bear so to speak. Until you can, and you must, deal with them, your "success" in trading will be fleeting.

For example, let's say our baseball player is now entering his sixth year of performance. Instead of the sixth year turning into a probability year based on his past five years of 0.280 RBI, his RBI drops to 0.190 because events during that year affected our player's performance. So, deviations can detract from probable performance. Only the player may ever know the reasons for his poor performance, and he must deal with them if he is going to attempt to improve.

As a professional trader you must train yourself to be geared toward probabilities. A successful trader knows that if you duplicate your trading success from yesterday you will continue to make profits. This is probable.

However, if you deviate from the norm, you will enter the realm of possibilities, where you can make a lot of money in a best-case scenario or where you might not be able to make profits and instead wind up losing for the year.

If you have fine-tuned your trading strategies to make profits on a consistent basis, then the possibility of catastrophic losses will be diminished.

What about strategies in the marketplace that allow you to make consistently small profits when you are right but, which on the flip side, will cause you to suffer big losses when you are wrong, albeit inconsistent and infrequent? Most unsuccessful traders implement these strategies without realizing it. One strategy, which involves selling out-of-the-money call and put options with several weeks left for expiration, will generate consistently small profits for 11 months of the year. However, in the 12th month huge losses generally mount, not because you cannot control your losses, but because your strategy of selling options premium never addresses the need to take losses! The selling of the premium consistently will make money for you because the premiums erode to nothing. There is no need for you to "take your loss" because there are no losses. Instead of honing one of your most important trading skills—taking reasonable losses in case you are wrong—you wait for the expiration of the options to "close" your open trades out.

Watching premiums erode is not trading, but more money management; it's part, but not all, of the equation for successful trading. Unfortunately this strategy does not also require you to "take small losses and let profits run," which are key to successfully speculating in all markets. When your short premium positions go against you, and they do one month out of twelve, you won't know how to cut your losses. A lot of traders who use this strategy tell me they will cut their losses when the time comes. However, what happens if the trader doesn't get the cushion of the eleven months of profits but gets hit in the first month of such trading strategy? These traders will spend the next eleven months trying to get back to even! A tough way to make a career out of "trading" in this manner.

When you take a look at probability plays versus possibility plays, go for the probability plays, which will increase your chances of survival in the trading business. Even within this context, there are plays which give the impressions that you are playing with probability, not possibility—case in point is the selling of options premiums. The only plays skewed in your probability favor are the ones which demonstrate "cutting your losses and letting your profits run."

RULE 3

Choosing Convenience Means That You Have To Pay for It

The most popular items which appeal to the general buying public have always been packaged for convenience to save the buyer time, such as prepackaged foods. One by-product of this packaging for convenience is to remove the need to make additional choices. For example, if you like convenience, want to save time, and don't want to make choices, then you are the ideal candidate for the next salesperson pitching his or her products.

You pay for convenience. In exchange for saving yourself time, someone else has to use his or her time. If you eat your lunch at a restaurant, you save time by allowing someone else to prepare your food, but you pay extra money for not selecting your own food at the store and making your own lunch. Allowing someone else to buy your food and make your meal means that you have given control of a part of your life to others.

Convenience costs. When it comes to your success as an investor or trader, the cost can be high. Nowhere in the world is there a more expensive environment than in the trading and investment community where relinquishing your responsibilities is so expensive. For example, limited real estate partnerships and Real Estate Investment Trusts are legally binding creations for investors who want to take advantage of tax loopholes and tax advantages. Something as diverse as real estate property oozes convenience when packaged into neat little bundles of ownership, managed by people in different parts of the country and sold to armchair investors such as you and me. The packaging and marketing cost investors dearly.

I've always held the philosophy that I'm always my best analyst. However, I'm also prone to buying the time of others so that I can accomplish what I need to do with greater efficiency with the time that I have. I am particular about what I buy and know how much of my own time to contribute.

In the case of market analyses I buy the daily data from vendors. I use the same software that others use to take the raw data, and I reformat them into chart-type data. I use the same approaches that others use to analyze these chart patterns.

I differ from all others in the sense that after I take all the information I've gathered, using the same software and hardware that these traders use, **I always reinterpret the information for my own use**. Where many investors ask what others think and analyze and then execute along those lines, I do my own thinking and analyzing. You should, too.

My attitude is not that of a skeptic or a cynic, but of a person who knows what exactly to look for in information. Anything that deviates from my intended needs I dismiss readily. Anything that captures my interest and has the faintest inkling of validity or value I use.

To speed you along your path to successful trading and investment these are the things I look for from other analysts and traders when I trade or invest:

1. Has the trend of the markets I'm following changed? In others words, do others see signs of such changes that I don't see? If there are changes unknown to me, what are these people saying and how are they justifying those trend changes? Their reasons could be based on fundamental analysis, technical analysis or a combination of both. Once I track their lines of reasoning, I still reserve the right to make my own final decision. Where they disagree with my analysis, I leave these facts as an open and operating hypothesis. Until market action proves their analyses right, I do not integrate their approaches into my trading strategy.

2. Are there parallel markets which others are tracking which may give forewarnings of imminent trend changes in the markets I'm actively trading? If there are, then I need to track the best analysts in those areas so that I can get clues well in advance of the trend changes in the markets I'm tracking. For example, I might be trading the airline stocks. Since I personally don't have the time to track other markets, I will follow analysts who specialize in related travel-type industries: trucking industry, the oil industry, and the hotel industry. I do this so I can find reversals in trends in these other markets which will affect the airline industry directly. For example, I track the oil industry for a lookout on what I expect the airline industry to do. When oil stocks start to rise, the professional oil analysts and their investors expect the price of the raw materials to rise, i.e., oil prices increasing. This eventually increases the profit margins for the oil companies and their related service companies. However, rising oil company prices is the death knell for airline stocks because the price of the main product that airlines consume—air fuel—will increase and cut into the airline industries' profit margins. This is only one of many "peripheral" industries I track to obtain a better forecast for the airline industry. In the process of tracking so many industries it does bog me down. I have yet to be able to find shortcuts to this in-depth method of analysis. Sure, I can buy the research and analysis of others, but by doing so I become dependent on others. Why don't I follow the airlines' analyst with the same diligence as the other analysts? Because I trade the airlines and I don't want to be dependent on these analysts, but rather the peripheral industries' analysts. The conclusions from filtering out all the noise from the other analysts are more valid than those drawn by the airlines' analysts themselves. This roundabout way to obtain valid signals works more often than it doesn't.

3. How badly off have these peripheral industries' analysts been? The eccentrics in the business are many, but every so often an eccentric will have such a radically different perspective that instead of being so deviant from the pack, he will actually lead the pack. (This is unfortunate since it forces me to continue to monitor everyone, especially those who have fallen into disfavor.) To dismiss these "bad" analysts would be similar to throwing the baby out with the bath water. You can't do this. Every piece of information has validity. As your own analyst, it is up to you to find the right time and environment for these misplaced bits of golden nuggets to flourish in. Most people will not spend the time to mine these bits of information to uncover the gold veins.

Once you've established an analytical environment in which you feel comfortable, your confidence in your own analysis will grow. This confidence should continue. There is no better feeling than knowing that you've been able to rely on yourself for the final outcome.

So choose with discretion the independence of doing your own analysis over the convenience of relying on others' analysis. You will reap sharper trading skills, reduce your risk of relying on others, pay less in fees by relying more on your own skills, and enjoy more trading success.

RULE 4

Trading Success Is a Slow Climb Uphill, but Trading Failure Coasts Quickly Downhill

Steven Jobs, one of the cofounders of Apple Computer, dropped out of college and developed the microcomputer in his parents' garage. Not everyone can do the same even if he/she has the "minimal" resources used by Steven Jobs, but those resources certainly can help.

The old joke went along the line that Jobs dropped out of Stanford and worked out of his parents' five-car garage. Stanford is a college, just like any college, but it takes some bucks to get through there. A garage is just a garage, but this is a five-car garage. It also takes some bucks and resources to need a five-car garage. He also had developed the skills to create the microcomputer.

In a similar manner so goes the success with trading. The overnight wonders you've heard about are wonders. Without infrastructure and substance these overnight wonders come and go. The money which was made so abruptly will not stay with the owners if they have not created a structure to maintain that environment, including the trading habits and patterns a successful trader must have.

I often hear of young traders going to the floor, taking $10,000–$20,000 and immediately making a killing of several hundred thousand dollars. When I hear these stories uttered by phone clerks and runners I merely shake my head in genuine sadness. The manner in which these young traders make their money, that of grossly violating sound trading rules and practices by overtrading and taking huge risks, will be the very same way in which they will lose all their profits.

The sword cuts both ways.

Seldom are those who have the wisdom to fall back to sound trading practices and rules after they have made a killing in the markets. They all waste it away.

You and I hear of those who have gone on the floor to trade with no money and parlayed them to huge profits. Yes, these people do exist but they are far, very far, and few, much fewer, between. They are the exceptions to the rules. In any profession, in any career, there are those who are stellar performers by sheer effort. But if their success is to be sustained you will find upon closer inspection that they probably were borne into their professions and are the second or third generation of such representatives, they had support from mentors, they had built some support infrastructure, they had developed good trading habits, or some combination.

Then there are the "stellar" performers because of circumstances. If there are no support infrastructures they will soon fall back to their previous level. If someone makes a lot of money in the markets very quickly without any experience, the chances are very good that the money will be lost unless the trader leaves the business and retains the money.

In 1969, a theory of career development was developed by a teacher, Laurence J. Peter. It was called the Peter Principle and was explained in Peter's *The Peter*

Principle, William Morrow publishers, copyright 1969, coauthored with Raymond Hill. The crux of his observations showed that people progress to their level of competence in life and then, having found this level, they stagnate there forever. At their "Peter Principle" level, these promoted people deliberately but unconsciously find failures surrounding them in their new responsibilities and task to prevent them from further advancement.

However, this principle doesn't explain ongoing failure in these people's careers. Over the last several years we've seen many corporate heads get tossed out. The same has occurred with many recognized athletes. This stuff makes headlines in tomorrow's newspapers. Why has this been the case so recently?

Enter the Eng Principle

I offer another principle—the Eng Principle. The crux of the Eng Principle explains why people fail, not what happens that prevents them from progressing beyond a certain level of competence as the Peter Principle explains.

In a nutshell, the Eng Principle points out that *people fail in careers because they naturally gravitate back toward their own best level of competence from which they should never have been projected.* Unlike the Peter Principle which indicates that *people move up* to their level of competence and then display incompetence, the Eng Principle indicates *people move down* to their level of competence and then most often disappear from view.

In the case of the Peter Principle, accolades and successes surround the career of the observed person. With the Eng Principle, failures and recriminations surround the career of the observed person.

I bring up the Eng Principle because I have observed it happen countless times in the trading business.

Unlike any other business in the world, the trading business has the most immediate gratifications imaginable: If you make the right decision, you are immediately rewarded; if you make the wrong decision, you are immediately penalized.

By pointing this out I want you to know why you have not been able to continue in your successful trading. Yes, the fault partially rests with you because you are not aware of the different environment in which trading is conducted. The primary reason why there are so many apparent failures in trading is related to the immediate reward, and punishment, nature of trading itself.

Let's compare the real world and the world of speculation.

In the real world, i.e., not the trading world, a career person accumulates knowledge of his or her area. With skill and training the person achieves expertise and succeeds in that area.

Let's say that the person has moved slowly from the mailroom of a large corporation to a successful vice-presidency of the personnel department. This person's career path shows a natural evolution of obtaining greater and greater responsibilities. This is the Peter Principle in action.

Now, let's take the same person who is now the head of the personnel department. Through a merger or acquisition of the corporation by a larger company this vice-president is now made an executive vice-president of international sales of the larger entity. Most observers would consider this to be a fortunate happenstance. What a lucky break! What additional income and status!

I say, "What an environment for automatic failure!" I guarantee you that this new executive vice-president of international sales will have growing pains, relearning of tasks from different perspectives, implementing new management skills, and a myriad of other responsibilities and performance requirements of the new position.

In most cases like these, these candidates will eventually fail. This "promotion" now starts the horrible path of failures and recriminations. Unless this international salesperson is a quick-study and devotes countless hours away from the office to pick up the knowledge that he would, and should, have picked up had he progressed in the natural path, he will fail at his new position.

We've all seen this happen time and time again. For example, how many actors and actresses have become overnight successes only to disappear from public view after successive flops?

We can say the same of some of our athletic heroes. Although they achieved athletic success, many have failed to their level of competence in their personal lives. The sadder fact is that we, as members of the public, have had to see these specific athletic successes unravel in front of our eyes when these same heroes could not adapt to status and monetary rewards.

What does this mean for traders? In the context of seeing the Eng Principle in action in the real world, the reader will recognize that traders are no different. In fact, in the trading environment, i.e., the world of speculation, the punishments are swift and eviscerating. Through the vagaries of market action, instant fortunes and resultant "heroes" have been made.

Overnight political actions have caused markets to jump favorably for traders. Assassinations of leaders and geopolitical turmoils have caused short positions to profit. Traders positioned, most often unknowingly, to take advantage of these market-based vagaries have benefited handsomely. (Does history make the human, or does the human make history? In this case, it's history making our human, the trader!)

Most who were not structured well to begin with eventually lost all these profits. These market losses through malevolent actions didn't even have to be attributable to the markets. Most such fleeting-fortune traders, however, thinking that by being there at the right time thought also that they were privileged forever. Not so.

You've got to earn money in the markets to be able to keep it from the markets. For example, if a trader who takes on large position risks makes a bundle of money, he will eventually lose it all because the manner in which he made the money will also be the way in which he loses it all. To earn money in the markets you must trade conservatively with your capital and limit your equity and position risks; when your positions start to show profits you must let those positions run up. Even if you correctly "earn" your money, you have no guarantee that you will be able to keep it if you venture outside the trading arena. I know of some who ventured outside the trading environment with their profits only to lose it all on failed investments; a lot more lost money than made money outside the trading environment.

One of the smartest retired traders I have seen knew that a three-million-dollar fortune he made in the 1987 crash was a fluke. Prior to this he was a struggling trader. At the ripe old age of 24, he was still struggling to be profitable as a stock option trader. He was positioned on the short side prior to the 500-plus-point drop in the Dow Jones Industrial Averages. After the October 1987 crash, his positions exploded to over three million dollars in profits. He took his money, waited for his leased seat to expire, and then quit the business. Then, he started a business refurbishing antique cars.

Seven years later, after a night of cruising on Lake Michigan and then partying at North Pier, our group of traders, brokers, and other assorted types had breakfast as the morning sun rose. I asked this 31-year-old retired trader point blank if he missed the trading environment. He replied that he didn't miss it and was glad for his fortunate episode. He explained that he always knew he wasn't that good of a trader. He knew he was too young. The business of trading did not interest him. In 1987, he saw a phenomenal amount of money accrue due to no fault of his own. Instead of then trying to learn the business with his own money, which by then was a small fortune, he decided that he wanted to spend his life doing other things. And that's exactly what he did. He knew his weakness, and the freedom he got from the profits allowed him to instead go into other areas where his strengths were.

So when you see a young trader make a lot of money quickly, look underneath him to see whether he is standing on the rock of Gibraltar or on overextended stilts. The rock of Gibraltar took centuries to develop. Stilts are the results of merely nailing several two by fours together.

In the former case, continue to monitor him and then plunk some money down. In the latter, keep an eye on him and wish him well for he will need it. Then be on your merry way.

What the reader has discovered is trading success is similar to any other profession: time must be spent in acquiring the knowledge for success. Trading is one particular business where a trader, without any knowledge, can make a small fortune just by being in the right place at the right time. However, the stellar successes of such traders are rare. Given enough occurrences of trading opportunities such a trader will eventually lose it back to the markets.

Even though the reader might not be professionally inclined to be a trader or professional investor the reader now knows how to uncover the "successes" of these professionals. Some very successful money managers are: Templeton, Soros, Lynch, et al. You can immediately benefit from the sound successes of trading and investing by investing money with them. Those who are flukes of market whims have had their days in the sun and have gone.

RULE 5

Break away from the Markets, Market Letter or the Newspaper— and Do Something as Simple as Thinking. Do This Especially When You Encounter Market Losses

As automatic as successful trading must become, at times you need time to remove yourself from the market environment. Then use this time away to regroup your thoughts. This often happens when your trading and investment activities encounter a series of losses.

When you are trading well, this is what is happening: Your approach to trading is in tune with the market stage and the market's stage is in tune with your trading methodology.

When you are trading poorly, this is what is happening to you: The market is bigger than we are, in all its aspects. We often attribute our market losses to changes in market conditions. Additionally, it is so much easier to blame conditions external to ourselves for bad outcomes. When your trading results in losses, effects and methods are no longer synchronized with results and outcomes. You must put a hold on your trading and sit back and think. Think!

You must find out if the losses you are now encountering are the results of a change in your methodology or a change in some other factor. If you notice that you've tampered with the length of your moving averages, varied the markets you are trading, looked at quick ratios from a different length of time, or traded other industries, etc., then you must return to your original conditions. These are the conditions which made you money.

Once you get back to your original trading conditions, you must analyze why you deviated from them. For example, why did you shorten your moving average from 13 days to 5 days? Or, placed more emphasis on M1 monetary indicators than on M2? Or, traded the financial futures, which are new to you, instead of the grains which you have a record of making money in? Or, traded the biotechnology stocks instead of continuing with the auto stocks? I am not against growth for surely your shift to other markets, your adjustment of your technical indicator parameters are indications that you are growing into new markets, new approaches. But you must still approach these new markets, new parameters with the same guidelines you've always used when you were successful in trading the markets and parameters you have gotten use to. You don't want to get into a new environment with new sets of tools and approaches until you are ready to do so. Always use the old tools, the old approaches on the new environment. It's only after you've seen how the old approaches and old tools work in the new environment that you then fine-tune the old approaches and tools for the new environment.

Tracking the reasons for your problem is very difficult since they are deeply imbedded in your earlier conditioning by your environment. This problem is based on earlier conditions, and because it's now so hidden in the past, you've most likely forgotten the roots of this earlier problem and need to delve deeper to uncover it. It's a problem based on environment because the current environment you are in is supportive of this "wrong thinking."

The current environment is constantly in flux. It shifts all the time. Your constant approach, with its markets you've traded and its stable technical indicator parameters, has suited you well for successful trading. Now, if the current environment shifts somewhat, your previous approach will be inappropriate for current market conditions. If you were to shift your approach and or parameters to adjust to this current environment you must make sure that the shift is warranted. How do you know that this current environment shift is only temporary, i.e., once it works its way through, it will return to normalcy? If this is the case you would then find that your changing of the markets traded, and the shifting of your parameters, would have made you suited for success in a temporary market. You would then be likened to chasing the constantly shifting winds, never ever able to capture them.

This current environment continues to reinforce also the long-forgotten roots. When should you shift or not shift your markets or your parameters? There are no hard and fast rules which, if violated, would flash a signal to you that you should adjust for a different environment. The only indicator I know which tells you that your approach must be changed is the indicator based on money: when you start to lose money, that's when you must seriously consider shifting and adjusting. Don't deceive yourself into believing that other indicators are appropriate, i.e., an increase or a decrease in the number of buy and sell signals based on previous parameters; this indicator is formulaic and is not based on money. It's going back to the old adage: hit 'em in the pocketbook, where it really hurts.

23

Tracking the roots of your problem is similar to attacking the many-headed mythical Greek monster, the Hydra. All the heads emanate from one body, but they are attacking you from all sides and are distracting you from concentrating on and attacking the one source, the body, that will enable you to remove all the heads.

Your reasons for doing what you do in the markets are varied at this point of your life, but they all emanate from some primary source. Seeking out that primary source will be more efficient in attacking the problem or problems that prevent you from successfully trading.

Most traders never analyze their problems far enough to find the primary reason. So, they never get to an opportunity to use their successful methodologies again. At this point of the thought cycle, these traders attribute their losses to supposed changed market conditions. **The truth is they have tampered with a successful methodology to insure losses**. Only you, the trader, can know the reason.

If you've ascertained you have not changed methodologies and are now encountering losses, then by process of elimination, you must conclude that the market's cycle has changed. You can do nothing to prevent this from happening. For once in your attempt to force blame of your unsuccessful trading to outside conditions, you are now vindicated. I personally have always found it difficult to make money when trends are shifting from bearish to bullish, or vice versa from bullish to bearish. As with all other traders, I take my lumps.

If you encounter a new market environment, you must now modify or scrap your methodologies to accommodate the new shift. Do this as a final answer to your increasing losses. Do not do this as an initial answer since the market's condition does not change that often; as individuals, we are more fickle and change more often than the market's trends will change. The stock market's bull cycles can last 10 years or more; bear markets last shorter. It would be difficult to say that your bullish trading strategies for the last ten years of a bull market cycle gave you losses; more likely you tampered with your methodology during the course of the ten-year cycle. In commodities, bull and bear cycles are shorter, but in relative terms commodities are the same as in the stock markets.

So when the losses in your trading account start to mount, you are most likely wrong, not the markets. You might be philosophic and respond that these losses are only temporary, or that these losses wouldn't be losses if trade executions were better, or if the Moon hadn't squared Pluto on that day, ad absurdum. What you and I do know is that these losses are there and affect your trading equity. Trading equity is your lifeblood to on-going success.

If these mounting losses you have begun to accrue are not accountable by your original game plans then you must stop whatever you are doing and:

1. Evaluate whether or not you've changed the trading methods. If you find that you have changed your trading methods, then you must uncover the reasons and recognize them. Then work around them.

2. If you have not changed your methods, then consider the possibility that the market conditions have changed. Be honest with yourself when you have ascertained that the problem doesn't rest with you but with the market conditions. If this is the case then you must apply different methods to the markets. When you apply different methods, be aware that you are now essentially starting the whole process again; this entails the use of conservatism, proper risk, and money management.

You will find many varied reasons for the ways the markets perform because they are compendiums of human interactions. They are continual and ongoing. When you find that you are no longer in synchronization with the markets, i.e., you lose money, sit back and evaluate the situation according to the prescribed approach suggested earlier.

Only when you feel comfortable with your new assessment can you, and should you, resume trading.

RULE 6

Market Manipulators May Play on a Rule of Speculation after It Has Become Established

This rule basically says that any rules that are currently in use in the markets eventually become the focal point of counter strategies by some pretty sharp market operators.

I found a bunch of rules years ago and worked them into my trading strategies. Some of these were applications of Elliott Wave theory, Gann square points, Fibonacci retracements levels, etc.

When the public became sensitized to these strategies the strategies worked somewhat less successfully. They worked, but I had to modify them for each situation. For example, if I saw a market retracing from a high move, I immediately forecast a possible retracement value. At first the retracement would coincide exactly with the forecasted values. After a while they would just sell off just slightly past these forecasted values. Then they would just ignore the forecasted values and blow completely through them.

I adapted to the situation by shifting my stop loss orders, at first from one tick to two ticks to three ticks to finally five ticks in certain markets. I had to modify my parameters throughout the markets.

After trying for a while to second-guess the market and the application of these methods by practitioners to the market, I just stopped and told myself that what I was doing was stupid. I had lost track of what I was supposed to be doing and allowed the analytical approach to force me to change my trading style! The tail now wagged the dog.

I had to reorient my thinking: I needed to have long positions in bull markets and short positions in bear markets. I had taken this initial premise to profitable trading and had executed it in the marketplace, using technical indicators that would flash buy signals in bull markets and indicators that would flash sell signals in bear markets. Any other signals muddied my approach. Unfortunately with the ease of making money in massively bullish markets and massively bearish markets I had become lax and looked at indicators which shifted me away from my initial premises: I started to look at mildly bullish signals in trading markets, for example. I shifted my parameters and traded other markets which were neither bullish nor bearish. Still I found trading success with these other markets and other parameters because of my ability as a fast-thinking trader; my honed skills as a trader made profits for me. As I deviated further away from my initial premise I found it harder and harder to make profits using the now changed parameters and less discriminating view towards market conditions. In retrospect, these eventual losses were directly attributable to losing track of my original premise.

In the meantime, the markets and their players had adapted to the methodologies that I first used. The methods were being used by many others. As long as others did not use my approach, I could stealthily use mine. But when others jumped on my bandwagon, my approach no longer worked.

I never thought I would actually say that these methods would be corrupted by their popularity, but I am saying this now. My current solution to this dilemma is to avoid talking or writing about innovative or novel trading approaches unless the public is already aware of them. Then I feel more comfortable discussing those approaches.

The other approach to using methods which are now less effective because of their popularity is to patiently wait out the application of these methods by their practitioners. As time passes these practitioners will find that their approaches no longer work because everybody else is using them and they themselves will no longer use them. Somewhere in this "disenchantment cycle" the abandoned methodologies will have an environment in which they can become effective again.

This second approach presents several problems. The first problem deals with the time needed to "wait" out a methodology to expend itself. It would probably be accurate to say that two generations of traders need to come and go for a methodology to pass through this disenchantment cycle. Once these practitioners have retired from the trading environment it is time, once again, to "rediscover" these methods. For example, the Elliott Wave was rediscovered by Robert Prechter. A modified form of "tic volume" was rediscovered by Joe Granville in the form of On-Balance-Volume. Edwards and Magee in the late 1940s rediscovered chart patterns from Wyckoff, and Wyckoff rediscovered chart patterns from the strategists before him.

Nothing is original in *our* latest "discoveries." There is, however, uniqueness in their applicability in current market situations.

Prior to the rediscovery process there are those among us who will fade the "forecasts" of these methods.

The market manipulators are those who will buy just slightly ahead of the Fibonacci retracement numbers, sell one or two days in advance of the Gann time squared forecasts, or get a jump on everyone else by selling immediately after the right shoulder of the Head-and-Shoulder pattern forms.

To rectify these problems I sat back and wondered what I was really trying to do with these forecasted numbers.

After throwing away all the excess thought patterns and trading methods that had been built around the original forecast methods, I concluded that these methods were originally designed to forecast imminent reversal points. Now they had been corrupted by market conditions and market players, so they were no longer valid.

This being the case I wondered if I might not want to stay out of these markets till all these manipulators had had their days in the sun, i.e., I enter the markets after they have had their plays. What do I give up? The possibility, not the probability, of buying on the low of the retracement or selling on the high of the rally. Was this important to me? Not being able to buy the low or sell the high? I concluded that it was not. I could wait till the manipulators had had their play, wait till the markets had possibly gone past the forecasted reversal prices or times, and then step in. If the markets did not go past where the manipulators had entered and test the reversal points, I would miss the opportunities to buy low and sell high, yet I would have even more assurances than the approximate, forecasted reversal points were more valid!

I turned this perceived problem into an even more sound analysis of market conditions! For this I gave up not buying the bottom or selling the top! In return I received a higher probability of success in my trading and investing.

How was I able to increase my chances of successful trading by not trying to buy the bottoms or sell the tops? Markets do top out and they do bottom out. Look at a chart of some stock you have tracked in the past. Where has it bottomed out or topped out? See how fewer times the markets show a top or a bottom but how much longer the markets are moving AFTER they have bottomed or topped out? This indicates that the chances of getting on board an upward move is greater once the move has started than it is trying to find the bottom to the market to buy.

A less personal, but more recent incident involving the S&P 500 Index illustrates these points. Named the "S&P Game," the strategy involved buying a stock that was close to being added to the Standard & Poor's 500 Stock Index. In the past when a stock was added to the S&P 500 Index, it tended to rise five percent after inclusion. Because of this tendency, the game was to buy the stock prior to inclusion and unload the stock after the five percent increase had been made. Many brokers and traders tried this strategy.

In the past, the S&P would add the stock to the index after the close of business for the next day's inclusion. Traders and investors would analyze which stock was the most likely candidate for inclusion using the publicly known S&P parameters for inclusion. Because of the perceived disadvantage to index funds, who were forced to buy the added stock after the announcement, the S&P moved the announcement time period to at least one week prior to the add-date. The S&P hoped that this would allow the index funds enough advance warning so they could leisurely add the stock prior to the upward movement.

However, the problem was that people who were not professionals could now play the game of buying the stock one week before the add-date. This brought in more buyers, thereby creating wider price movement.

Microsoft stock jumped 15 percent between May 12, 1994, the S&P announcement date, and June 6, the add-date (this news was announced three weeks in advance); the extra time allowed more nonprofessionals into the game.

Now that the public has gotten wind of this relatively easy way to make a larger return, the hint that this will no longer work has surfaced. S&P announced an addition—United HealthCare. On June 30, 1994, the add-date, the stock declined 2 points from the previous day, and a total of 4½ points since the announcement date. As a result, many brokers and traders suffered losses.

It never fails to amaze me how little games like these that try to take advantage of nuances first of all are not the correct way to make money in the markets. These nuances exist only for the time that the differences exist. Once they close up, or disappear, you can't make any more money with them. It would be much wiser to learn the correct way to trade and trade for longer periods with more opportunities.

Learn the proper rules and logic of correct trading. These little games offer diversion, but not a core method of profit-making.

RULE 7

A Stock Is Not Always a Great Bargain Because Its Yield Is High; a High Yield Often Indicates Price Instability

Every so often at a party someone will ask me what I think about a certain stock. For the most part I tell them I really don't know that much about the stock and try to change the subject of the conversation courteously. The friends stay in the room nursing their drinks, but the relatives persist and follow me out of the room asking, "Why don't you know anything about it? This stock is yielding 12.2 percent while the rest of the industry is yielding 3.4 percent. I think this stock is a good buy!" Mumbling from my defensive position behind the door, I go into a 15-minute explanation, which, by now, is pretty standard to open their eyes to the facts about the overemphasis on dividends.

A more appropriate title for this chapter should be: "There Are No Such Things as Lies, Just Different Perceptions of Time."

Let's take a look at what is used to create the yield number for stocks. Yield consists of a ratio between two numbers, one a numerator and the other a denominator. The numerator is the dividend paid out by the company in the last quarter. The denominator is the current price of the stock.

$$\text{Stock's Quarterly Yield} = \frac{\text{(Last Quarter's Dividend)}}{\text{(Current Share Price)}}$$

Note the adjectives I've used in the last two sentences: "last" and "current." With these two separate time frames I can now distort or create a different reality.

Dividends are paid out quarterly. The amount of a dividend is a culmination of the previous operations of the company. So, for the rest of the quarter no other dividend number is reported, and no other number is reportable.

The price of a stock is current. Its price, volume, and trading activity are reported daily from the exchanges and recorded in your financial newspapers.

The problems arise when we look at yields not on a quarterly basis, but from other time frames: half yearly or yearly. To obtain half-year yield numbers, we add the last two quarters (this is never used to evaluate yield for stocks). To obtain yearly yield numbers we have to add up the previous four quarters of dividends.

Once we either have individual quarterly dividend numbers or summated yearly dividend numbers, we are left with another decision. Do we divide these dividend numbers by the current stock price, or some average yearly price of the stock? It's important to compare like to like, not like to what appears to be like.

When we compare dividends to price, we are most often not really comparing like to like; we are comparing apples to oranges. However, this erratic method of comparing yield numbers is acceptable, so beware of the following distortions: the past dividends are fixed, the current pricing of the stock in question is not, but instead fluctuates. The yield number resulting from comparing these two sets of numbers is an inaccurate way of determining actual yield. Let's take a look at how this can be so.

When a stock's current price drops, the dividend number is still fixed until the next quarter's dividend number is reported so the yield number will rise proportionately. (The best way to determine the forthcoming quarter's dividend would be to obtain industry analysts' estimates. These estimates are not recorded in the daily price quotes sections of your newspapers, however. Additionally you have to follow the stock to be able to readily access the analysts' earnings and dividends forecasts. Unfortunately, most of us aren't in this position.)

Let's say that the dividend for the first quarter of the year is $0.50 per share. Not only this, the dividend has been at $0.50 for at least the last four quarters, or a total of $2 per year in dividends. To obtain an annual yield number we will obtain an approximate average stock price for the year which is $58 per share. This average price of the stock may or may not be at or close the current pricing; it really doesn't matter since we have taken the full four quarters, or full year, of dividend payments. The annual dividend yield on the stock is $2 divided by the average price of the stock, $58, or about a 3.4 percent yield.

Now let's say the current price of the stock drops (note I indicated the current stock price and not the average stock price for the year which cannot drop precipitously). The annual yield of the stock will now rise dramatically. What problem has entered here? The current price of the stock has dropped while the last quarters' dividend payments have been reported and continue to remain fixed. This is a simple problem I've pointed out here and you would expect the newspapers to be so discriminating in the reporting of the yields, wouldn't you? Well, not quite so. In order to save time in calculating numbers, the newspapers only use current stock pricing, regardless of how different current pricing is from average pricing, to derive the annual yield of the stock from the last four quarters' dividend payments.

If the stock's price drops, the yield number will rise and often rise dramatically. Let's say the stock's price goes down to $50. The yield now rises from 3.4 percent to 4.0 percent, or $2 yearly dividend divided by $50 current stock price. If it drops to $30 per share within the quarter, the yield will go up to 6.7 percent. The unsuspecting public who reads the daily financial papers will happen to hit upon the stock that is suddenly yielding a phenomenal 6.7 percent when its industry is yielding a normal 3.4 percent. What a great buy they think. However, as we have seen this is the wrong approach for buying stock based on dividend yield.

The message is clear. Dividend numbers are fixed for a relatively longer time period than the pricing of the stock. Because of this lead-lag in pricing of the stock and reporting of dividend numbers, the unsuspecting public investors are often unaware of the distortions that can occur.

The problem to the investor is nonexistent if the dividend remains fixed at the $2 per share level because then the high yield based on the current stock pricing is accurate and does actually reflect a phenomenal bargain. However, this is not the case most of the time. If the price of the stock drops, then the fundamental condition of the company has changed, i.e., reflected in fewer sales leading to fewer revenues leading to fewer profits and finally, ouch, leading to fewer dividends.

How does the smart investor guard against being misled by these dividend yield numbers? First, you must be suspicious of yield numbers which deviate from the industry norm. If you find such a company, do a quick rule of thumb analysis.

Check the range of prices for that particular stock for the year, which is the last 52 weeks of activity. If the current stock price is below half the range of the year's price activities, the investor knows that the price of the stock has dropped dramatically. (Note I said that it has dropped dramatically, as opposed to saying that the price of the stock has stayed at the lower half of the year's price range. How do I know this? The dividend yield is higher than the industry average!) This conclusion warns the investor that this stock's dividend yield has risen dramatically not because of increased dividends, but because of decreased stock pricing.

The following scenario is possible, but not probable. If the price of the stock is in the upper half of the year's range, then several things are yet to be concluded. The first one is obvious: the dividends have increased and the price has not accurately reflected this fact. In this case, buy the stock. This situation doesn't often happen, and the following numbers and analysis will tell you why. Our previous example showed a stock paying out $0.50 in quarterly dividends to reflect a dividend yield of 3.4 percent. To get a higher dividend yield with the price of the stock currently at $58, the last quarter's dividend payment must be higher than each of the previous three quarters—considerably higher. The quarterly dividend payouts are: $0.50, $0.50, $0.50 and D, where D represents the last quarter's payout of $0.50. To get a higher yield out of these four numbers where the first three numbers have already been recorded, D must have to be high enough to overcome the burden of the three lower numbers and also high enough to have an impact on the yield number.

Let's say we are considering buying the stock with a dividend yield number of 6.6 percent annual yield instead of a 3.4 percent industry yield. How can this happen? To get 6.6 percent out of a cumulative dividend number for the last four quarters divided by a current stock pricing of $58, the cumulative dividend number must be a whopping $3.82 (so that we can have $3.82 divided by $58 to obtain a 6.6 percent dividend yield). If the first three of the four quarterly dividends are at $0.50, or a total of $1.50, then the last quarter's dividend must be $3.82 minus $1.50, or a whopping dividend of $2.32. If the $2.32 is viable, this means that the most recent dividend must show a whopping increase of 464 percent from the previous quarter's $0.50 dividend: from $0.50 to $2.32.

Between you and me, if the company is going to kick out a whopping 464 percent increase in the most recent quarter, I'm sure that even the management's cleaning service would have already gotten an idea of the bullish prospects for the company. They would certainly be closer to management than you or me!

This initial warning flag—dramatic rise in yield— should tell the investor to be wary of buying the stock. However, if upon further analysis the investor finds that the probability of the dividend decreasing is minimal (which then leads to another set of analyses), then the current drop in stock pricing is the aberration and the investor can conclude that pricing would rise again. In this case, the investor must buy the stock.

RULE 8

You Need Purse, Pluck, and Patience; Your Broker Needs Conservatism, Common Sense, and Conscience

What often confuses the investor or speculator is that his or her goals and the broker's goals are entirely different from each other. Because of these different objectives, the investor or speculator must know what to do to protect his or her interests and still be able to work well with a broker.

The investor or speculator is looking for profitable opportunities in the markets through capital gains or some form of dividend payouts, both of which have to be better than average. The broker on the other hand is looking for investment ideas, which may or may not be reflected in benefits to the investor or the speculator. The ideas are then reflected into transactions made by the investor or speculator. Transactions become commission dollars to the broker. And the broker makes commission dollars regardless of whether or not the client makes profits. To compound the problem, prospective clients outnumber existing brokers. If a client loses money and leaves the trading/investing game, the broker just picks up the phone to prospect for another one.

In a more business fashion, we classify each of these groups into either the *buy-side* or the *sell-side.* Investors and speculators are lumped together into the buy-side. Brokers are put in the category of sell-side. They sell you ideas, and you buy the ideas; that's all there is to it.

With these different objectives, you, as an investor or speculator must have purse, pluck, and patience, and you must find a broker to take the other side: conservatism, common sense, and conscience.

(If you find a broker who has purse, pluck, and patience, one of you is not needed. So to what avail is this chapter, you might ask? Possibly because you need to find a broker whose qualities fit well with your traits and skills. Complementary traits are not easy to find.)

A *Forbes* magazine article, dated June 7, 1993, quotes Frederick E. Rowe: "Warren Buffett continually exhorts corporate managers to think like owners. Similarly, we should seek out stockbrokers who think like investors." Slim chance.

Successful investors and speculators exist who are advanced and have developed all six qualities. These self-reliant investors make money consistently. Until you get to this point, you must find brokers who are your complements.

Let's go through each of these qualities that you as an investor must have as prerequisites before you can successfully invest in the markets.

1. First is the issue of having purse. You've got to have the money to play the game. No money, no entry ticket. Of course, this is money you can afford to lose, not money you are counting on to live. Now, having enough money just gets you into the arena of playing the game, but it doesn't insure your profitability in any sense of the word. Even after you have the money to get into the game, you must keep from losing all of it. No money, no

40

entry ticket. Lost money? You get kicked out of the game. No question about the way this game works.

2. The second prerequisite is pluck. You must have the nerve to act on your convictions. The development of determination and confidence reflects the amount of understanding you have of the markets. With less experience, you have less confidence in your ability. As you play the game longer, you develop awareness of what can happen to you, and you do not allow these events to crop up. Once these safeguards are in place, you can trade with greater confidence.

Those of you who have not yet gained much experience in the marketplace need to develop pluck, especially those who have been getting nailed in the markets. With such experiences, the investor becomes more timid and more adverse to risk taking.

The investor's timidity is resolved only when he or she absorbs enough confidence, knowledge and maturity from losing (making mistakes) and gaining (acquiring wisdom).

Until the new or experienced investor comes to terms with what caused the losses, he or she will repeat this scenario over again.

3. The final investor prerequisite is that of patience. This skill is the hardest to learn but not because it is hard to understand. We already understand that nurturing and developing requires patience. Instead, we have a hard time developing patience because we have a limitation: We are limited in our physical time on earth. We are not infinite and, therefore, have the greatest concern for the passing of time. We are finite, our existence will end someday. With this impetus on us to make better use of our time, we are naturally impatient when confronted with situations that need time to develop.

From my own personal experiences I have realized that I have to wait for the rest of the investing world to catch up to what I was able to see in advance. I do not have an exclusive monopoly on foresight. On the contrary, we all have that ability. Even if you have the intelligence and resources to analyze market situations correctly, you still need the other prospective investors, the world in a universal sense, to find your analysis valid and then execute on it.

If you specialize in one aspect of market analysis to the exclusion of anything else available, you will become an expert in that area. If you propound on your area you want others, who are considerably less involved, to immediately pick up on this. This is desirable but unrealistic, possible but not probable. Others have their own priorities and agendas. You must allow them time to absorb your insights. This demands patience on your part.

For example, if you've analyzed and have decided to buy a particular stock or commodity contract, you will want to establish a position in it first. Then you will have to patiently wait for the rest of the world to discover what you have discovered earlier so that you can profit when you sell to them at higher prices. **Waiting is the hardest part.** We all want to be vindicated. Those of us who don't have the patience will lose patience and rid ourselves of stocks or commodities positions well in advance of the rest of the investor world's participation.

Only when the world participates do we get our payout!

Brokers' qualities are different. In fact they are somewhat complementary to your own successful traits. Brokers need to be conservative, have common sense and conscience.

1. Brokers need to be conservative. In this role they have to be the voice of reason to dampen your often unwarranted enthusiasm about certain market plays. As a relative novice to the business of the trading and investment world, you pick up ideas all the time. You're constantly on the prowl for profitable situations. From your perspective every idea that is market related is new to you and must be acted upon immediately. A wizened broker has seen all of what you are seeing today. Over the course of his or her lifetime in the business, he or she has seen more than enough ways those market ideas can part you from your money. The good broker will tone you down and get you back on an even keel so that all these supposedly great profit-making opportunities will go by the wayside and not part you from your money. The good broker will be able to filter out most of the bad ideas and focus on the few remaining good ones which can turn into profits.

A good friend who has never traded the markets got into trading at the end of 1993 and continued to trade into the first three quarters of 1994. At this juncture of market action I cautioned her about the volatility of the markets. She proclaimed that her profits were annualizing at an exorbitant rate, and she wondered why I, a market veteran with over twenty years' experience, hadn't done as well as she had. I had nothing to reply since I knew that she was right.

She took the risks that I would not have taken, so she reaped the rewards that I did not earn. The equation was balanced; it was very fair.

I was cautious enough to get her involved in some heavy action stocks so that she could focus on that action toward the end of 1993 and early 1994. Because she focused her attention on a handful of stocks that got a lot of press, she did not have the time to find other situations to get her into trouble. I had tried to talk her out of continuing to look for "growth stocks" all to no avail, so this was the best I could do for her. She had flat profits that year. This was a time for any investor to be out of the markets. Unfortunately, in early 1994 investors in general got into the markets like lemmings going to sea. Anything they bought in early 1994 has shown losses as of this date. It was a difficult year.

Caution is the result of many years of experience. A good broker will temper the exuberance an investor has

43

for entering or exiting the markets at the wrong time or for the wrong reasons. Thankfully, most good brokers are more cautious than they are exuberant.

2. The second trait a good broker must have is common sense. A simple trait, but surprisingly lacking in some brokers. I have seen the way the markets have evolved over the years by using their respective marketing strategies to unload securities and commodities on the public.

After so many years of watching inexperienced brokers operate, I am no longer amazed to see these very same brokers get caught up in the very same games that are foisted on the public. To have one investor want to buy a stock on the high of the move because of a bullish news article is sad. But for this investor and his broker to chase this very same market up is worse than sad— it's a tragedy. At the time that temperance of risk must be used, the broker is running amuck with the clients.

Some brokers have argued with me that the clients want to trade and often trade situations with unknown risks. If these brokers don't take their business, they argue that other brokers would surely take them. To this I really have no insight or suggestions except that even these risk-prone brokers will eventually also lose these clients.

3. The final trait a good broker must have is conscience. Please don't confuse this concept of conscience with our narrow concept that companies must have ethical and moral prerequisites similar to the investors' own morality. This type of thinking and investing is highly unrealistic and has no place in the markets because money has no conscience. So why should investors personify the marketplace in similar fashion? We play for keeps in the markets. To personify the markets and to treat your money with such emotional content is to create environments where proper trading and investment techniques cannot exist.

I personally look for situations where such "do-gooders" have indicated that they won't invest or trade. Some very interesting and profitable situations exist. I merely view these as plays to be made, not moral decisions to live by.

What I do mean by conscience here is the one your broker has toward you and yours. The broker must not view you as a commission generating resource but should look upon you with a conscience geared toward your benefit. The conscience-oriented broker must look first to you to find out what your needs are, not what his or her needs are.

It is only when you find a broker whose first purpose in dealing with you is your benefit will you have an edge in the markets.

The market is a battleground between the very intelligent and shrewd operators of the world. Make sure that you have a good broker as an ally before you enter the fray. Nothing is worse than feeling betrayed by members of your own camp when the enemy is attacking you in battle.

One quick, effective way to help you determine the quality of your broker is to find out whether or not he or she still has clients from the first year of entering the business. If the broker does have some of these original clients, you can conclude with a higher probability that he or she has served these clients well from day one. If, on the other hand, the broker tells you his or her clients vary and the oldest clients have been with him or her for less than several years, be aware that this broker has managed to stay in business by constantly soliciting new clients because he or she may not have done his or her job as a conscientious broker maintaining current client equity.

Most investors who deal in the markets have in the backs of their minds the apprehension that they are members of a herd of sheep. Unless and until you get out of that category, a sheep you must remain.

RULE 9

There Is Less Pressure To Sell at the Top Than Ten Points Down from the Top; There Is Less Inclination To Buy at the Bottom Than Ten Points Up from the Bottom

This set of observations of human behavior, as modified by the price of the underlying investment, shows what our inclination is when prices are at the top and when prices are at the bottom. It implies a set of actions, or rules, which will prevent you from becoming successful in your own trading.

We make the observations. What then? Are we to buy at the top or sell at the bottom? Not absolutely, but with conditions. How, then, are we to counter our natural inclinations?

To go against the natural inclinations we have, and what others who think and act similarly to us also have, we must be contrarians. We must act contrarily to the markets by trying to sell at the top and buying at the bottom.

If market player classifications were so easy to pigeonhole, we would all be very good writers and very good traders. Let's pause a bit and try to determine what contrary opinions are. What is a contrarian? First, what is contrary opinion? Is it quantifiable? Is it qualifiable? Contrarians are defined as:

> "An investor who does the opposite of what most investors are doing at any particular time. According to contrarian opinion, if everyone is certain that something is about to happen, it won't. This is because most people who say the market is going up are fully invested and have no additional purchasing power, which means the market is at its peak. When people predict decline they have already sold out, so the market can only go up. Some mutual funds follow a contrarian investment strategy, and some investment advisers suggest only out-of-favor securities, whose price/earnings ratio is lower than the rest of the market or industry." — Barron's *Finance and Investment Handbook* by John Downes and Jordan E. Goodman

When the markets are charging into new highs, we find that we get caught up in the fever of the bullishness. Because of this we are insensitive to the fact that the market is most likely at the end of an extended runup.

The same situation exists with the markets making new lows. When the markets are plummeting to new lows day after day, we find ourselves in a very bearish frame of mind. Instead of looking for value we look to bail out of our losers. These thoughts that run through the mind at moments like these are not needed and do not contribute to successful trading.

Contrarian thinking, as a concept, is valid. However, as a trading tool for timing entry and exits, it's terrible. It's not quantifiable. There have been attempts in the past at trying to gauge this contrarian mass psychology, which are still currently used: bullish and bearish sentiment indicators. From a larger, global perspective the shift in mood of such indicators can be used to interpret when the mass investing public has shifted in investment focus. The successful interpretation of such shifts is reflected by strategies that go against the masses than by going with them.

If you are to behave and act contrarily, you must subjectively decide for yourself what the base sentiment is at the time you start to apply this contrarian perspective. Once you have developed a baseline of sentiment, any shift will provide you with the beginning, but not ending, of the interpretation process. Where the interpretation ends and where you will act is the problem area: we really don't know where it will end because contrarian sentiment has never been quantified well enough to allow practitioners to gauge its shift accurately.

The ideal situation is to remove yourself from trading environments that can disrupt your thinking, i.e., set yourself up to trade in environments in which you have full control. Instead of looking to buy on the highs you must first be long at the lows. With a previously established position prior to the resultant move to the upside you will be less inclined to want to go long at the top since you already have a position. In fact, you might want to sell out your longs. Similarly if you are short before the markets punch through to new lows you will be less inclined to want to short on the new lows.

There's a bit of a twist here. What this suggestion—already be long at the lows expecting the market to punch to through new highs and already be short expecting the market to punch to new lows—implies is that you've already incorporated some sort of contrarian attitudes already. Why else would you want to be buying on the lows, instead of selling, or selling on the highs, instead of buying? (The key to knowing whether or not you should do either of these is based on what you analyze the main trend of the market to be. If the market is decidedly bullish, buying on lows, i.e. corrective retracement lows, isn't similar to buying on new lows in decidedly bearish markets. In the former case, the market will punch to through new highs; in the latter case, the market will only go lower after a bounce up.)

This then is the correct approach to applying contrarian thinking: only use contrarian thinking to close out already existing positions which were established with other parameters! At the lows, you use the gauge of value. At the highs you use the gauge of technical overbought indicators (selectively, of course; for further discussions see *The Technical Analysis of Stocks, Options & Futures* to assess when overbought is valid and when oversold is valid).

But you never should use contrarian thinking to enter into new positions, which most uninformed traders would do. Here again is their indiscriminant use of trading tools or methods at the wrong time or stage of market activity.

Don't mistake what I'm saying with the old saying that you must buy new highs or sell new lows because this saying does not contradict what I just said, but is only the latter part of a two-part strategy: buy low first to initiate positions then buy higher to add to your positions (see *Trading Rules*, Dearborn Publishing, copyright 1990 William F. Eng for additional thoughts on this rule).

RULE 10

Beware of Shorting Worthless Stocks: Do Not Forget That Dust and Straw and Feathers, Things with Neither Weight nor Value in Them, Rise Soonest and Most Easily!

Most people who don't have an idea of shorting often pick the cheapest stock to short. This is the worse thing that can happen. *Shorting* either stocks or futures is the process of selling these assets before owning them with the intent of buying them back at a lower price in the future. This is the opposite of first buying assets for eventual sale. The ideal stock to pick to short would be the one that is overextended on a runup, regardless of pricing.

Let's address why this is the case.

One of the basic arguments propounded by people against shorting stocks or commodities is that the price of the short can only go to zero, i.e., a finite profit. The price of any stock or commodity, however, can go to an unlimited price on the upside, i.e., a long position can benefit from an appreciation that is potentially infinite. Given these two possibilities, why do professionals still short the markets, especially higher priced stocks or commodities?

The professionals only short two types of stocks: stocks which are on the highs of their extended runups or absolutely (here again is the issue of subjectivity: what does "absolutely" mean?) bankrupt stocks which have no chance of becoming profitable. There are many more that fall into the first category than the latter.

The time period to hold the short positions is also considerably less than holding outright long positions. If you took a look at the times that an open short position lasted versus one for long positions you will find that it is at the ratio of less than one to five.

A short position must be profitable much more quickly than a long position; otherwise, the professionals immediately close out the positions. At low prices, the chances of the price coming down dramatically is slim to none. There is some sort of value established by the public on the worthless stocks of at least a dollar or two. It will take a long time for $2 stocks to drift to less than 25 cents in value, even if the company is bankrupt. To go from $2 to $0.25 the short would have made $1.75, but the price had to drop 87.5 percent.

At high prices the situation is different for shorts. A 100-dollar stock price could dip to $95 in a blink and still only be considered to have lost 5 percent of its value. In a similar situation where the price drops to $98.25 to make $1.75 on the short, the percentage decrease is only 1.75 percent.

The chances of a stock fluctuating 1.75 percent, regardless of pricing, rather than 87.5 percent is much greater. The probability of profitably trading shorts rests with shorting the higher priced of the two if the absolute dollar moves are the same for both high priced and low priced stocks.

In the first example, there has to be a fundamental change in the stock's condition to justify a $1.75 drop. In the second, high-priced stock issue, a 1.75 percent fluctuation is par for the course in its daily trading—a mere technical condition.

RULE 11

A Short Interest Slows a Decline and a Long Interest Slows an Advance, but Neither Will Permanently Prevent a Movement When Intrinsic Conditions Are Radically Changing

No matter what technically goes on in the markets, the fundamentals affecting those markets must be taken into consideration first. I've seen this happen in stocks, in futures, and even in real life. In real life I've dealt with quality people and the results have always been quality. I've also dealt with others whose behavior forced me to watch my back all the time. It's much nicer to deal with quality people. At least you don't have to sleep with one eye open all the time.

This rule stipulates that even though technicals may affect the stocks temporarily, there is no getting around the core of what those stocks are. If the stocks are fundamentally bad, there is no way to avoid them being bad. Similarly if they are good, the intrinsic value will show themselves.

In stocks, blue chips are always blue chips. No matter how badly they get beaten up, they always show their true qualities. There are some major exceptions such as International Harvester, now known as Navistar International, and Johns-Manville Corporation which will probably never come back. These situations are results of conditions beyond their controls.

Technically, if the stock has a lot of interested buyers who have already bought the stock, they will prevent the stock from going up. Who else will buy the stock to push the price up? Same with too many people interested in shorting the stock. Short interests create a captive audience of potential buyers. They have to cover their shorts by buying the stock they are short. Hence, a protracted decline is not in store for these stocks with heavy short interests.

My warning is that if the fundamentals warrant bullishness, then the stock will go up. The same is true with the stock being bearish; it will go down with or without the extensive short interest.

In the interim, bullish stocks can and do go down if too many people are already long the stock. The same can be said of bearish stocks going up if too many people are already bearish on those stocks. The built-in group of shorts in such stocks will act as a support group of buyers if the stock dips ever so slightly. If buying such short stocks can push investors slightly to the buy side, you will find that such stocks will move dramatically higher. Similarly if too many people are already long a fundamentally good stock, the stock, based on technical merits, will have a hard time going up until the excess longs which overhang the market are taken out.

So if your analysis of the particular stock is decidedly bullish, then any setback is only temporary. Once the temporal problems are cleared away, the stock will resume its upward move.

RULE 12

Fools Can Take Profits, but Wise Traders Know When To Take a Loss

Let's discuss why we emotionally cannot take a loss when all practical considerations point out that we should and must.

When we close out open trades that are profitable we feel very good. We know that the profits will be translated into benefits for ourselves. It's the reason why we strive to trade the markets. We want to make money from them.

We can get into trading positions which result in no profits and no gains. Hence, we trade and trade and realize that we aren't making any profits, nor accruing any losses. We dismiss this experience as ongoing learning and hope that as time progresses we will not waste any more time on taking on positions which don't make us money. These trading positions make no money for us, but they don't do what losing positions do to us.

However, the other side of the trading equation is that more often than not our trading positions result in losses. These losses always start out as open trade losses and only when we close them out do they then become permanent losses. The losses do not create warm feelings because they prevent us from making money and instead cause us to lose money. We now don't even make money: we lose our money. This happens when we don't trade well.

One of the ironies of trading is that most of us do not talk about our losses. We talk about our winnings with vigor, however. We hide our losses; we are ashamed of them as signs of our failures. People perceive our judgment as defective when they know that we have sustained losses. This explains why I never talk about either my losses or winnings. Because I don't talk about anything I do in the markets, I face no embarrassment, nor do I have victories to regale. This is my attempt at trying to maintain a balanced perspective on being able to control losing situations professionally.

Once I talk about my losses to others before I close them out to realize the losses I find that I eventually have to justify them to others. Even if I don't have to justify them to others, others will come to me and ask for an accounting of my losses. They deserve no such accounting since they are not my bosses.

I have become my own self-sustained trader. You should be striving for this also. Until the time comes when you are tight-lipped about your trading prowess and weakness you will need to talk both about your winners and losers to others. It's natural for us to communicate our desires and ambitions to others when we are in the process of acquiring them; it's a form of goal formation. We create goals of attaining success and diminishing failure by verbalizing our desires and ambitions. The more we can create an environment which supports our pursuit of these goals the more successful we can become.

My advice is never to talk about your winners or losers. But you might say that if you never talk about your winners or losers, especially losers, you will never find the solutions to eliminate the losers.

This is a valid objection. If someone other than me can prove to me that they have a better approach to the markets than I have, then let them give me enough information to whet my interest. Once intrigued, I will pursue the knowledge. I don't think they can. And this is the exact approach you should take toward all these newfangled ideas and techniques to better and more consistent profits.

Have I taken the path that I caution you not to take? Yes, I have. I believed once that what others taught or professed to know was more than what I knew. For a period in my early development as a trader, I followed up on all the talk and advertisements of products and services claiming that they would reveal their secrets if I merely paid several hundred dollars. At the beginning the knowledge I acquired was beneficial since my knowledge of the markets was limited, but as I learned more and more I realized that the people knew less and less. I became more leery of buying these products and services. After I discovered that what most of these people considered to be secretive I actually already knew but applied somewhat differently, I concluded that these purveyors didn't know any more than I did. Still, I paid to learn that basic fact.

What does my experience of learning that the experts didn't know more than me have anything to do with you being a wise person to take losses? I became a wiser trader after I realized that I already knew what these people thought they knew when it came to market knowledge.

I paid to find out that they knew less than me. This was very critical in my self-discovery process. After I realized that these experts who were successfully managing money or writing best-selling market books or consulting with huge financial institutions didn't know more than me, I concluded that whatever I was seeking to know, it was not necessary in order for me to be as successful as these people were! This was the revelation to me. But, until I went through this actual process I couldn't come to the conclusion that I already had all the knowledge for successfully trading the markets!

The only missing element was being able to put all the bits and pieces of knowledge into one cohesive plan of huge success. This missing element struck me one day in a brief flash of insight.

The act of taking a loss when your judgment is wrong is market wisdom in action. By itself this act is negligible in impact, but in the context of a trading career, this singular act is highly symbolic of your success as a trader. The act of taking losses when your judgment is wrong implies many things about the person who is trading. Some of these are:

1. You are humble enough to admit defeat in face of market dictated reality. Your positions turn into losers regardless of how well you've analyzed them. The fact that you get rid of them implies your admission that the markets are bigger than you, which they are.

2. You view the markets as ongoing and that you can come back tomorrow, the next day, or even a year from now and still trade successfully. You know that you can always get back into the markets because you've accepted the fact that your current losing trade must be closed out because it is not behaving according to your forecasts. This gives an element of faith that what will be will be.

3. Taking care of losses first is the key to market participation longevity. Fight and run away, to trade another day.

4. You understand that taking losses is not the polar opposite of taking profits. Taking losses is only used to manage your losses, not make money. The act of taking a profit is a profit-taking action, and not the act of preventing a loss. You are wise

enough to know that the act of taking a loss is not a profit-making action, but a way to prevent further loss. The profit-taking action adds to your equity, but the loss-prevention action doesn't add to anything.

5. You've wised up to the real game of trading.

Learning to take losses is not as simple as just telling your broker to get rid of the bad trades in the marketplace. To get to the point of taking losses as a matter of fact requires a depth of understanding of market action. Once you've realized that developing the ability to take losses when you are wrong is one of the first critical steps to your market success you are indeed a wiser trader.

RULE 13

Traders, Speculators, and Investors View Markets Differently

What perspective do you have in the markets? You must identify yourself from the perspective of being able to see what you do. Three types of players compete in the markets and they mustn't be confused with each other: the traders, the speculators, and the investors. A trader is like a baseball player with a long schedule of games; a speculator is like an oarsman, who after long preparation rows one important race; and the investor is like the ticket seller who, without interest in the contest takes the gate receipts. Which one are you?

The traders have many more opportunities to get into the markets than the speculators or the investors. The traders have no bias toward which direction to trade the markets from: Long or short, it doesn't matter. They will take whatever positions will show the most likelihood of profitability. Their strength rests in the fact that they have created or found an environment in which they benefit from much volume of activities. Because of these broader parameters, they can easily evaluate several hundred opportunities during the course of the week. They can be scalpers or floor specialists. The "upstairs" traders who pay close to wholesale commissions costs don't have access to all orders so this category is a hybrid located closer to the traders than the next category of market players, the speculators.

The speculators, on the other hand, have fewer opportunities, but much more depth of knowledge of the fewer opportunities than the investors have. They are essentially a specialist in their area. Their strength in successful speculation is based on the timing of their positions. An additional strength is that they can monitor many more markets than the myopic floor traders or scalpers. As a general rule more markets to follow mean more profitable opportunities. They have preselected the markets they want to follow. From this shortened list of candidates they track the developments of each of these items.

The investors just buy and hold, not short and cover. The majority of people fall into this category. Their two strong points rest in their ability to allot to investments capital that they don't need and their ability to hang onto positions. In being able to put up money they can afford to lose, they are not pressed to obtain an immediate return on their investments. This allows them the luxury of finding growth stocks and latent bull moves in commodities. The second strength, that of holding their positions, is very crucial in making the profits. This presumes that they are holding onto winners! Most unsuccessful investors will hold losers and hang onto them.

What about a hybrid investors/traders type? The best type of profit-making people would be those who treat losses with a trader mentality—getting rid of them quickly. The same hybrid traders also treat winners with the investor type mind—hang onto them as long as possible. Most of us react the other way: We get rid of winners quickly and stay with losers longer!

These hybrid traders are exactly what successful traders do. They mix and match and extract the strong suit of each category and create the right environment for themselves so that they do get rid of losers and hang onto winners!

Several years ago, I befriended a person who did exactly this. In the early 1940s, he had inherited $40,000 from his parents (no, this is not John Templeton whom I wrote about in my first *Trading Rules* book). Since it was an inheritance which came from nowhere, it was found money. He did not need the money and he did not spend it. He was in the position of treating this money from an investor's viewpoint: buy and hold. This was an ideal situation for him to be in since he wasn't self-trained as a trader early in his investment career.

The stock he bought and held was Tampon Brands, now called Tambrands. Needless to say the buy-and-hold strategy has benefited him handsomely. He is worth several million dollars on this simple, but elegant strategy: buy the strongest stock in an industry and stick with it.

The only element of luck that entered into this scene was that among his first pick, he picked a horse that won the race! But this luck didn't carry him through to the other races as this person was wont to tell me. None of his other investments panned out as well as this one. He did acquire enough insight to be able to develop profitable, short-term trading strategies.

He now has branched out to trading other markets. He trades the futures markets, of all things, with finesse. He was kind enough to send me his trading statements. Note in Figure 13.1 that the statement ended on August 31, 1990, with a realized profit of $52,632.60 plus open trade profit of $11,875.00 for a total profit of $64,507.60 (commissions taken out) on a forward balance of only $16,935.75, or a percentage gain of 380.80 percent for the month, or annualized at 4,570 percent! Talk about jumping from the frying pan into the fire; this man went right for the market-action jugular. Note that what he learned in hanging onto Tambrands has made him a successful hybrid trader.

That's the beauty of knowing how to trade successfully. Once you learn the right habits and strategies you can trade anything from anywhere in the world, just as this investor/trader did. He learned the value of long-term plays with his Tambrands stock; then he branched into the short-term speculation arena. He was successful in both areas.

This is truly the most enjoyable career that I know of; believe me, I've done a lot of things in my life. Hence you too must become a hybrid trader: Trade short-term with losing positions and invest longer-term with winning positions.

Figure 13.1 shows a copy of the account statement that records all opened and closed transactions for this trader-investor. Note that the account started the month with $16,935.75 and ended the month with a profit of $69,686.16 (commissions are not deducted) plus open trade equity on 20 US Dollar Index contracts of $11,875.00 for a total of $81,561.16.

Figure 13.2 is a copy of the reporting forms our trader/investor filled in every month for the contest that he had entered, "Financial Traders Association" quarterly trading contest. Note the account was started on March 22, 1990, with equity of $7,110, and he had shown a net profit of $82,978.00 by the end of August 31, 1990, for a return of 1,167.1 percent for the three-month trading period.

Figure 13.3 shows the commodity which made the bulk of the profits for our trader-investor. It is a copy of the chart our trader-investor provided me so I could analyze how he had come to the conclusion to pyramid the September 1990 Canadian Dollar contracts to the bullish side. He used basically conventional chart analyses patterns and trend lines to justify his long positions.

FIGURE 13.1 Account statement

CLEARING MEMBER PRINCIPAL COMMODITY EXCHANGES

MONTHLY COMMODITY STATEMENT
ACTIVITY AND OPEN POSITIONS

PERIOD ENDING
AUG 31, 1990
ACCOUNT NUMBER

OK

10-17-90   SEGREGATED ACCOUNT   Contest A/c

DATE	BOUGHT LONG	SOLD SHORT	COMMODITY/OPTION DESCRIPTION	PRICE	DEBIT	CREDIT

THE CHICAGO MERCANTILE EXCHANGE, SEVERAL CHANGES HAVE BEEN MADE IN
AGRICULTURAL MARKET CLOSING TIMES FOR CERTAIN HOLIDAYS. THESE
CHANGES WILL MAKE HOLIDAY CLOSING TIMES IN THE AGRICULTURAL QUADRANT
CONSISTENT WITH THOSE IN THE INTEREST RATE AND CURRENCY QUADRANTS AT THE
CME. THESE CHANGES ARE EFFECTIVE OCTOBER 1, 1990. PLEASE CONTACT YOUR
TRADING DESK FOR MORE DETAILS.

DATE	BOUGHT	SOLD	DESCRIPTION	PRICE	DEBIT	CREDIT
-31-90			BALANCE FORWARD			16,935.75
-31-90			RETURN SUGTRBK DESK STAND	CASH		50.00
-03-90	2	2	SEP 90 C-DOLLAR	P&S	106.40	
-10-90	10	10	SEP 90 C-DOLLAR	P&S		10,488.00
-21-90	20	20	SEP 90 C-DOLLAR	P&S		21,086.00
-22-90	5	5	SEP 90 C-DOLLAR	P&S		2,834.00
-23-90	15	15	DEC 90 NY SILVER	P&S		542.00
-24-90	20	20	SEP 90 C-DOLLAR	P&S		1,436.00
-27-90	5	5	SEP 90 US$INDEX	P&S		559.00
-29-90	5	5	SEP 90 US$INDEX	P&S		134.00
-31-90			INTEREST EARNED AUGUST 1990	CASH		67.81
-31-90	25	25	SEP 90 US$INDEX	P&S		15,650.00
-31-90			ACCOUNT BALANCE -- SEGREGATED FUNDS	....	....	69,686.16*

NET REALIZED PROFIT OR LOSS FOR MONTH   52,632.63

O P E N   P O S I T I O N S

DATE			DESCRIPTION	PRICE		CREDIT
-24-90	3		SEP 90 US$INDEX	85.48		2,055.00
-24-90	5		SEP 90 US$INDEX	85.50		3,375.00
-24-90	5		SEP 90 US$INDEX	85.83		2,550.00
-22-90	5		SEP 90 US$INDEX	85.56		3,225.00
-30-90	2		SEP 90 US$INDEX	86.18		670.00
	20*		OPEN TRADE EQUITY	86.15		11,875.00*
			TOTAL OPEN TRADE EQUITY			11,875.00
			TOTAL EQUITY			81,561.16

FIGURE 13.2 Reporting forms

SHEET TO ACCOMPANY MONTHLY STATEMENTS
(please xerox and submit one such sheet with each statement)

8/31/90

Your name or your contest entry name (as it is to appear in Barron's). Please list the division entered (stock, etc.), the duration of the contest (one year or four months), and indicate if you are a broker or a registered advisor.

FUTURES, 1 YEAR, ADVISOR

Please give one telephone number here if you wish to have your number listed in the standings.

YOURS

Please indicate the day you entered the contest if you entered late.

Market value of your contest account (includes idle cash, etc.) as of the close on the day prior to the start of the contest (This information should appear on the statement preceding the first month of the contest. (Late entrants give market value as of the close of the day they entered.)

1) *7,110*

Please list the dates when cash was added or removed from the account and the amounts involved.

	date	amount
CASH ADDED +	*3/22/90*	*— 10*
CASH REMOVED —	*4/16/90*	*— 33,908*
0° c*	*6/18/90*	*+ 25,341*
	8/1/90	*+ 10*
••••••••••	*(NET REMOVED)*	*— 8523*
8,561• +		
8,527• +		
90,088• ◊	nbers in the amount column to determine a) the amount of net cash added (removed) and b) the maximum amount of net cash added to the account.	
7,110• —	: the following amounts of cash are added to the account: $4,000, −$3,000 and	
82,978• ◊	/ords, $4,000 is added, $3,000 is removed, and $1,000 is added. Then the net cash	
	;3,000 + $1,000 or $2,000. The maximum amount of net cash added to the account at	
82,978• ÷	).	
7,110• %		
1,167•060478 +		

..., ...ing market value for contest purposes. This is the sum of line 1) plus the maximum amount of net cash added to the account at any point.

2) *7,110*

Compute the total profit in the account, which is the profit shown on the monthly statements (increase in market value from the start) minus the net cash added. *8/31/90 EQUITY 81,561+ CASH*

3) *82,978*

REMOVED 8,527 = 90,088 − 7110 = 82,978

Divide line 3) by line 2) to get the percentage increase.

4) *+1,167.1 %*

Name and telephone number (toll free if possible) of an individual at your firm which can verify the above information. (Brokers list their branch managers.)

_____ phone __,_____

Financial Traders Association, P.O. Box 7634, Beverly Hills, California 90212-7634 • (213) 305-9300

FIGURE 13.3 Chart provided by trader-investor

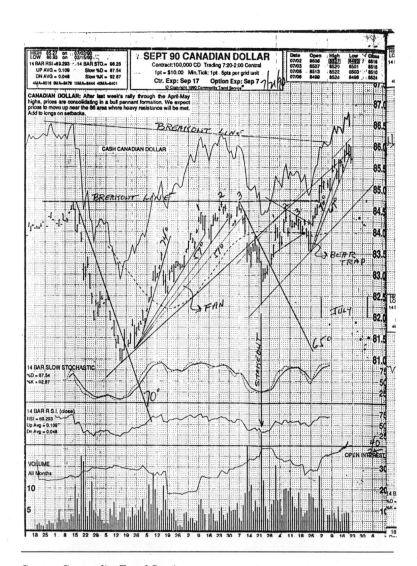

Source: Commodity Trend Service

Note that in Figure 13.1 the play in the Canadian dollar made $36,368.00 (one trade of two contracts on August 3, 1990, showed a loss of $106.40) profits for our trader-investor, or about 43.80 percent of total profits.

Figures 13.1–13.3 showed me there are many ways to make money in the markets. In the case of the example with the Canadian dollar trades (see Figure 13.1) the careful reader will note that there were five closed positions in the Canadian dollars:

1. Two contracts closed on August 3, 1990, for a loss of $106.40.
2. Ten contracts closed on August 10, 1990, for a profit of $10,488.00
3. Twenty contracts closed on August 21, 1990, for a profit of $21,086.00
4. Five contracts closed on August 22, 1990, for a profit of $2,834.00, and
5. Twenty contracts closed on August 24, 1990, for a profit of $1,436.00.

I am not able to discern what prices and how he went about making his trades, but I can conclude that he pyramided a bullish position on the way up. His chart analyses also indicated he expected to play the Canadian dollar from the long side for several reasons. He had inscribed on the chart a pattern he considered to be a "bear trap." Bear traps are market movements which deceive the observer into believing the markets are bearish, when in fact they will immediately reverse and become bullish. There are other inscriptions which pointed to the bullish frame of mind he had for the Canadian dollar.

In trade number one where he took a loss of $106.40 on two contracts I can conclude that he took an initial position as a test of the market's bullishness. When he discovered that he had gotten into the market a bit too soon, he sold the initial positions out at a small loss.

In trade number two he had already pyramided some positions. How and at what prices we aren't sure, but I do know that on a per contract basis he made only $10,488 total divided by ten contracts, or $1,048.80 profit per contract.

In trade number three he had placed 20 contracts on and made a profit of $21,086.00 or an average of $1,054.30 per contract, which is about equal to the per contract profit in trade number two.

In trade number four he had five contracts and made $2,834.00, or an average profit of about $566.80 per contract.

In trade number five he had on 20 contracts and made $1,436.00 profit or an average profit of only $71.80 per contract, which is a dramatic drop from trades number two and three.

What significance can I read into these numbers? First, I can deduce that he started to pyramid with two contracts and discovered he was too early so he sold them out. By August 10, 1990, he had accumulated a bulk of his long positions because on August 10, 1990, he had already started to take profits on part of his long positions. The largest average profit per contract is around $1,050 so we can assume with a high probability that by the time he started to sell out his positions on August 10, 1990, the biggest part of the Canadian dollar's bullish move had already been made. Toward the end of his campaign his average profit per trade dropped down to $71.80 per contract. Even though there was an average profit per contract on the fifth trade not all of the twenty contracts traded showed profits. I conclude with a high probability that the last few positions that he entered into his total long position started to show losses; that's why the average position per trade was so dramatically lower than the highest average profit per trade. By August 24, 1990, the bullish move in the Canadian dollar had already been made.

68

This campaign took only three weeks! Excellent trading. I couldn't have done better myself!

RULE 14

Narrowness Always Follows a Violent Market Move; thus, When Stocks "Mark Time," You Do the Same

One of the most boring things to do is to watch paint dry. I haven't actually sat down to watch paint dry, but at times life resembles this slow waiting. You've got to watch and wait. Wait and watch. Any combination, but not act!

The markets are often the most boring things to watch. Right now as I write this chapter, the Dow Jones Industrial Averages have been in a tight range of about 75 points for the last month. Boring. It looks like I'm watching oil-based enamel paint drying. It wouldn't be so boring had it been quick-drying latex paint.

Prior to this period of "marking time" of the market, the market dropped from a high of 4000 to a bit under 3600 in about a 5-month period. Some stocks dropped over 50 percent in value. Very few gained in value. A majority are down between 10–15 percent from their high prices.

Yet, as I watch the market chew around at this level, I've kept myself busy both within the markets by doing more research and outside by writing more books. This prevents my nerves from getting to me and playing games with my perception of reality.

Why is this so and what can we do about this? What little mind games must we play with ourselves to insure that we don't give back what profits we have accumulated? First you must transfer an observation you have seen in real life: for every action there is a reaction to the marketplace.

Markets move up. They move down. They go sideways or nowhere. There are no other patterns. Given these three types of market action, all interconnected and interrelated with each other in an ongoing continuum of market activity, you should know when to get into the market or stay out of it. Of course, there are strategies and plays that involve getting into market plays when most other players are out! These sets of strategies involve options, and I'll discuss the role of the option player later.

When a market moves dramatically from one price level to another, the market must need time to settle down. In the process of moving from one price level to another the market has upset the balance of ownership of stock. Those who bought stock at $100 are selling on the way down. When the stock hits a low enough level where active sellers are sold out, the market will rest and stabilize while the rest of the market players regroup and reassess their damage or profits. At $50 a share there are those who still own the stock at $100. If they haven't sold out at $100, they were surely selling on the way down. The market moved down to a level where all those who were holders of less conviction had already bailed out.

Now at $50 a share, the new price level itself attracts newer buyers into the markets to support the price, i.e., prevent the price from going lower at least on a temporary basis.

The early sellers were either sharp traders or else they had been buyers on margin and they needed to get out based on margin calls. Less frequently will appear sellers at $50. There are a small group of short sellers at this level. Whether or not they are profitable shorts is unknown by this type of market action. I can say with assurance that anyone shorting on the relative low of the move must either know something about the company or else is totally misinformed.

Once the ownership of stock changes hands at the $50 level, the price may or may not go back up. This all depends on the intrinsic value and the fundamental bullishness of the particular stock. In certain situations, the general tone of the market, either bullish or bearish, will be reflected in the majority of stocks going up or down. This particular $50 stock may be prone to the general movement of the market.

After the dramatic selloff comes the dull waiting period. Bullish forces must regroup to take the stock back up. Remember also that this resumption to the upside must take a longer time than it took for it to go down because the price territory from which the stock came—higher than $50—has left a lot of owners of the stock still "holding the bag." From $50 back up to $100 the strong bullish forces will encounter sellers. This is the additional reason why the stock must boringly build a base at the $50 level. The market has no other way to take out the "overhead" supply of stock from buyers and owners of the stock at higher prices. Until this supply is absorbed the stock will have a hard time going back up.

Many games can be played on the holders of the longs while prices are at such low levels. Bad news may be coming out about the company to panic these owners into dumping out their longs. Rumors may be flying of the company going under. The best strategy to shake ownership out of the hands of these losing investors is to allow their own fears to work on their nerves: let time pass without any news.

The informed speculator will look particularly at the base building for clues that there is "rotation" of ownership. By reading the tape and watching the bids and asks the speculator can discern when the informed buying shows itself more. Buying and selling are occurring during the base building, but as an informed speculator you want to see ownership of stock shift from bits and pieces to block buyers. The assumption is that block buyers are more intelligent traders and when they buy the prices will eventually go up.

The expectation is that after a base building period prices have a better than even chance of going back up. The resumption to the upside may or may not take out new highs, but the trader will observe noticeable movement to the upside.

So when prices are steady after a runup or a selloff, you must observe to see when the respective selling or buying increases steadily. Once you see this happen, you can mathematically presume that the price will reverse direction and you can get on board for the capital gains.

Note: In the case of options, you can take advantage of the boring, "waiting" period to your financial advantage. To take advantage of time, you sell premium and at the same time take on positions which will mitigate your risk in case you are wrong on the options you have sold. This is *spreading*. Option spreaders take advantage of the waiting periods by shifting the element of time to their side. Instead of letting time work against them, the spreaders sell options premium short and essentially allow the passage of time to erode the values of these options. In this manner the premium seller will receive the gain on the shorting of the options. At expiration, if all conditions are met (the options are not called away due to the option getting into the money), the premium seller would have gained from the passage of time. The real problem with this type of strategy is that spreading is more complicated, so I do *not* recommend using spreading strategies without additional study.

RULE 15

A Person Who Waits To Eliminate Uncertainty Will Keep Waiting

We can be prone to one of two faults. Some of us act too quickly, often without much thought or consideration. On the other hand, some of us act only after all the facts are in and only after spending considerable time deliberating these facts. Neither approach is really very good for helping you become successful at trading. The former is much better suited to trading the markets than the latter, but not by much however. Both faults are problems to success in trading or investment. Both are inappropriate to your success, but a melding of the two faults will be your salvation.

If you are a scalper you don't need to deliberate about every trade you make. You bid under the last sale and offer over the last sale. Do this two thousand times a day and you make a good living. Deviate from this method if you're a scalper and you are in trouble. Deep trouble.

If you are an investor you don't make a thousand buy and sell decisions everyday, but only a few during the course of a year. However, to get to the point of these few decisions, during the year you've analyzed fundamental numbers and technical reports thoroughly. Once fundamentals and technicals are right you step in with a commitment. Studying the numbers too much or trying to uncover more research will move you away from making profits in the marketplace.

Some wait until they are certain of everything. These people will find that they are subject to "analysis paralysis." They can't execute even though they have a buy or sell decision. Not too many fall into this grouping, but they are frequent enough for their complaints of lack of success to warrant mention in this special chapter.

Here is a good, practical solution to this quandary for these people: Once they do have what they deem to be enough information, they work with someone else to execute their decisions in the markets. This removes the immobility to action by taking out of their hands the responsibility of execution. Another person will do the execution for them. A friend who had this fault suggested to me that he was going to ask his wife to be his *offset person*—the person to execute his decisions. I thought about it and suggested that he look for someone with less involvement in his personal life. I sure hate to see a good marriage go down the tubes because of conflicts over trading! It wouldn't be the last time, but why set up a situation from the start that will endanger a relationship which can and should exist independently of trading?

Another solution, and this is literally playing mind games with yourself, is to trade only a portion of your total position when you have less than complete information. How, you might ask, are you going to accomplish this?

Let's presume that you need 100 bits of information before you buy 500 shares of IBM or 5 contracts of soybeans. If you get up to the level where you have 80 bits of information, you go in there and buy 200 shares of IBM or 2 contracts of soybeans. When the other 20 pieces of information come your way, and they still conform to your analyses, then place the other 300 shares or the other 3 contracts of soybeans on. In this manner you will have a partial position when you have what you perceive to be incomplete information. (The sharp reader will note that the second lot is larger than the first lot. Also, the investor is a buyer. You will ask whether or not I'm "pyramiding" correctly. This multiple positioning is not pyramiding but just accumulating a base position. In pyramiding bullish moves, you purchase fewer and fewer positions as the market gets higher and higher. This multiple positioning to build a base precedes the pyramiding mechanics. Once you have your 500 shares or 5 soybean contracts as a base, then you can pyramid.)

In this manner you'll be positioned, albeit less than 100 percent, for a market movement despite your prospective misgivings and still can take advantage of a full move on a partial position.

But what happens if you trade in only 100 share lots or 1 contract of soybeans at a time? These are contract sizes which are less than what's currently available. In the case of soybeans, or most of the commodity contracts, you can trade a small contract size of the MidAmerica Commodity Exchange and finish off your total position when you feel more comfortable with your information. In the case of stocks you can trade an odd lot, and round off the total position later.

In either case of stocks or commodities, you can enter your positions with full options contracts, which because of their mathematical components, offers you different effective positions based on their deltas. *Deltas* are proportionate movements of the price of the options based on the underlying stock or commodity movement and the options strike prices. (For a discussion on deltas, see *Options: Trading Strategies That Work.*

With this piecemeal approach to putting on a position, you should have no problems in developing a position in the markets.

You know that you have run into trouble if you find you cannot logically (in this case, it's really emotionally) find enough reasons to start even a partial position. This action, or more correctly, inaction, is an exemplification that something else is operating to prevent you from putting on a position.

Given what has been told you, you have a way to add partial positions with partial reasons. You now have no excuse to have no positions at all. But despite this approach if you find that you cannot put on positions, then I emphatically ask you to stop trading and take some time off to do much introspection.

No books or courses in the world can help since the subject matter dealt with in this book are all market-related. The inhibition is emotional and psychological.

RULE 16

Those Who Consider Wall Street as Strictly a Business Proposition Are the Only Ones Who Meet Success. What Is Marketed to the Public Is Something Less Than a Business but More of a Speculation

First, let me address the issue of this business being abundantly rewarding to those who treat this activity as informed speculation and not random gambling.

I appear on the Internet every so often and telecommunicate with the users throughout the world. (Internet is the electronic global information superhighway that has been developing over the years. It allows a person with access to a computer and modem to telecommunicate with others throughout the world.) One person entered a request for information from me. In this message the user asked what I thought about gambling and the markets. I responded that we all are gambling in the markets most of the time, regardless of what is said or written to the contrary. The user replied that he never regarded gambling as part of his trading even though he was taking flyers on stocks or commodities from friends and brokers with hot tips. He considered his approach to be more reasoned than gambling.

In essence we are always gambling all the time. We just analyze and find more reasons to lessen the gambling connotation perspective to the point we justify in our own minds that we are merely speculating with known odds.

There is a minor difference between gambling and speculation. Both require some sort of decision-making. Gambling smacks of helter-skelter decision-making. Speculation implies a more informed decision-making.

As speculators we know what we can control and what amount of capital we place into such risk situations. The ideal situation is to be an informed speculator in every transaction. This is also impossible to achieve. However, you can determine ahead of time what you will want to concentrate on, be it trading strategies or types of markets to trade in, and then spend all your efforts there. In this manner you aren't leaving the outcome of your objects of concentrations to mere chance.

Next, let me address the issue of how to treat this as a business and why you must treat this informed speculation as a business.

As a professional trader I learned to pace my expenses with my income from trading. Trading income, as a general rule, comes in "feast or famine" fashion. One day you may make thousands of dollars, the next day you can lose it and then some. The expenses, on the other hand, go out consistently. I had to be my own budgeting expert. The old-time traders have always taught me that if I can't pay for anything in cash I shouldn't buy it.

Let's discuss the income source and how you must budget your time and resources. As a manager of your own funds your objective is to obtain a consistent income from the use of your money by putting the money into risk situations. If you take positions which are too risky, not only will you lose your risk capital, you also won't earn any return; this forces you to take additional funds out of your remaining capital to cover your ongoing expenses. It's a double whammy when you lose capital in the markets.

So you must allot a certain portion of your capital for risk and a smaller portion for expenses. This is the downside to this problem of matching expenses with income. The good part of this is that once you get to the point of making more than your living expenses your investment returns may stay the same but the amount of capital you put at risk decreases greatly.

For example, when you start your career let's say you need $40,000 a year in income to live modestly. If you have $100,000 capital at risk you can make about $50,000 a year without a great risk to your original capital. At the end of the first year of trading you will have $150,000 less your $40,000 expenses, or a total of $110,000 to start trading in the second year. If you make 50% again, at the end of the second year you would have $165,000 less your modest expenses of $40,000, or a starting capital of your third year of trading of $125,000. Let's take this example out to the tenth year and let's see what you wind up with:

FIGURE 16.1 Sample Profit Table

Year	Capital at Start of Year	50% Return	Expense	Capital at End of Year	Net Profit for Year	Annual Return
1	$100,000	$150,000	-$40,000	$110,000	$10,000	10%
2	$110,000	$165,000	-$40,000	$125,000	$15,000	13.64
3	$125,000	$187,500	-$40,000	$147,500	$22,500	18.00
4	$147,500	$221,250	-$40,000	$181,250	$33,750	22.89
5	$181,250	$271,875	-$40,000	$231,875	$50,625	27.94
6	$231,875	$347,812	-$40,000	$307,812	$75,937	32.75
7	$307,812	$461,718	-$40,000	$421,718	$113,906	37.00
8	$421,718	$632,577	-$40,000	$592,577	$170,859	40.50
9	$592,577	$888,865	-$40,000	$848,865	$256,288	43.25
10	$848,865	$1,273,297	-$40,000	$1,233,297	$384,432	45.28

At the end of the tenth year, running at a rate of 50% return per year, with yearly expenses of $40,000 (for a total of $400,000), you will wind up with $1,233,297 in your trading account. This example does not factor in the income tax penalties on your starting capital every year. This also assumes that during the course of the ten years your yearly expenses do not surpass $40,000 a year, which can be pretty hard to do.

The imputed rate of return on your $100,000 over the ten years is an acceptable 28.56 percent per year return on capital. If your expenses are less than $40,000, or nonexistent if you have outside income, then your rate of return will go up proportionately.

The smartest way to put your $100,000 at risk is not to plunk it all down on one play. Instead, control your risk and manage portions of the capital in different risk segments. (See *Technical Analysis of Stocks, Options & Futures* for more on risk controls.)

The numbers, however, do not lie and they are realistic enough that you can do it, too. I've managed to do the same in my trading career.

Using the same forum, Internet, an informed user sent me a message illustrating how he methodically went about figuring out his business of trading. I reprint the message as illustration that he is currently concentrating on the development of his thinking process:

Subj: FUTURES AND TECHNICAL ANALYSIS

Dear Mr. Eng (WILLIAM.ENG@SYSLINK.MCS. COM),

I came across an article in the June 1994 issue of Futures magazine, and read David Nusbaum's article, "Cruising the Information Superhighway." Nusbaum described your attempt to solicit questions from Internet users about technical analysis, and that you were a veteran trader of futures. I have an interest in the futures markets, but found information and literature provided to the public is often generalized guesswork, and not very specific or practical, especially when rigourously tested.

I am a graduate student at U.C. Berkeley, and enjoy the use of a large body of work on investment. I have tried to devour as much as I could about technical analysis, but I understand that it takes experience in order to apply such knowledge.

Most of what I have learned is by experimenting and researching what seems to work and carefully dissecting what I feel is mostly bogus.

I have been trying to find a forum where I could discuss ideas that I have been working on, and to also learn more about trading and technical analysis from others who are much more informed and experienced. I have read your book, *The Technical Analysis of Stocks, Options and Futures* and have found it very enlightening.

I have tested a number of systems for the past year and a half and combined what seemed plausible and fundamentally sound, and tossed out ten times as much in terms of ideas I thought would work. This led me to test the systems on the computer with data reaching back for twenty to thirty years.

I eliminated systems that worked on only a few markets, or systems that did not work for long periods of time (i.e., during noninflationary times). What I found was the number of variables I was using tended to curve-fit the data (this is no big surprise), but when I used indicators, patterns and parameters that were not very sensitive or more robust, the systems started to work across almost all markets (though with differing degrees of success, but still with a net profit in almost all). There are added seasonal filters that I use for some markets, but the systems do well without them. I used very conservative figures for transaction costs and commissions, totaling $550 per trade ... I do this because the average winning trade length is 75 days and losing trade length is 10 days ... this may be overkill in slow markets or in very liquid markets).

I also found that the parameters for entry were far less important than for exit (this indicated to me the tough part about trading: exiting or staying with a position). I have started to trade the system in real-time, but (this shouldn't surprise you) I found that I second guessed two of the biggest trades this year (Coffee and Cotton, incidently and ironically, the only two that I overrode). I have ten open profit positions and eight closed positions, with only one closed position with a profit. (There is one open position in Coffee that I did not take, and one closed position in Cotton that I did not take).

Overall, what I started being comfortable with was with the systems that were longer term in nature, because they seem to work well across a broad range of market conditions; however, peak to trough account equity swings and volatility are large since I need to hold onto positions for extended periods of time. The equity curve for the system across about twenty-five markets is about the same fifteen years ago as it was last year.

I started, recently, to dissect each trade and find out why they didn't work, and I found that the ones that did not work were either ones in very choppy intermediate trends, or re-entry signals upon system exit. With refinements and trying to increase the methods of exits and re-entry I found myself simplifying the system even more.

I am wondering that you (sic), as a professional trader, you probably trade short to intermediate term moves instead of longer term moves??? If I choose to trade with a long term system, what methods could I use to lower volatility, aside from market diversification and trading shorter term? Could there be a strategy to trade short-term fluctuations within the longer term system signals, thus diversifying over time as well as markets?

Any help or insight you can provide me would be greatly appreciated.

Sincerely Yours,
Name Withheld

The Internet user had logically dissected his methodology and approached a portfolio of markets. He is well on his way to making a solid business out of trading the markets. He has what I consider to be obvious faults, but overall he is certainly a lot closer to investing success than a vast majority of people who are trying to become successful traders.

The obvious fault is that he "second-guessed" the two biggest moves for 1994: Coffee and Cotton. When a market runs like these two markets did in 1994 one of the worries an inexperienced trader has is he doesn't know how to move his stop sell orders or find a place to take profits. This is attributable directly to the fact that these one way markets are literally vertical and it is very hard to find a right price to enter stops or places to take profits. In upwardly trending markets it is easier to find price levels to take profits or enter stop sell orders—the previous knot of congestion before the move to the upside continued. In straight up markets there aren't any knots of congestions discernible on daily bar charts. That's why when you have straight moves you should look at shorter time frames to find some knot of congestion in prices so that you can enter stop sell orders or take profits when these congestion areas are violated on reverse price activity.

Note how well he has thought out his procedures and how he has sensitized himself to be particularly aware of certain things and activities.

You can certainly succeed in the trading business, but only if you treat this trading game as a business. Think things through. Plan carefully. Provide safeguards. Execute. Then examine results and revise if necessary.

RULE 17

Beware of Stock Splits That Can Create Strange Price Charts and Opportunities That Never Existed!

The stock market, and all its participants, never fail to amaze me as to what is created and foisted on the unsuspecting public.

There has been much written recently about what benefits or nonbenefits accrue to the companies creating stock splits or to the investors who buy the stocks of such companies in anticipation of stock splits. The articles basically show that investors holding stock before the split do not have an increase in percentage of ownership in the company, but the lowered pricing gives the shares more marketability. The issuing companies have also the same benefits. So, with the obvious reasons known why do companies continue to create stock splits? Are there more subtle reasons that we don't know about?

In a *Wall Street Journal* article, "Stock Splits Can Be Mere Paper-Shuffling" (October 13, 1989), Tom Herman, the writer, quoted Leon Cooperman, a partner at Goldman, Sachs & Co.:

"A stock split unaccompanied by a cash dividend increase is like giving somebody five singles for a $5 bill. You've got a thicker billfold, but it has no economic significance whatsoever."

This is not quite the case. My son, who just started to learn how to count, was duly impressed the other day when I showed him my wallet full of singles. This is exactly the game that is played in the stock market! Preposterously simple, but people fall for it all the time.

So, what is the story behind stock splits if we already know why they aren't that beneficial to investors? There must be something good to stock splits, otherwise why would they still be used so extensively?

I know of another subtle reason that creates opportunities for those companies that implement stock splits strategies. This reason has to do with creating opportunities that are never there. A form of revisionist history, so to speak. This is a clever way to distort reality, again. Let me illustrate this point with an anecdote.

Many years ago I tracked a company named Sherwin-Williams. I like the company: It has good fundamentals and good support from the buying public. And it's in an industry that is constantly needed: new paints. As usual I track the company for months, even years before I find the right time to step in to make a play in it. The company's earnings were dropping and the price of the stock was dropping. I waited for the stock price, not the earnings or dividends, to bottom out before I tested the water by buying some shares. After it stayed at around the $27 range for umpteen months I became distracted and made stock plays and business deals elsewhere. I stopped tracking the stock as diligently as I had been and merely looked at the stock in the newspaper's Sunday financial sections to recap what it had done the previous week. The stock did nothing. It stayed where it was and looked as if it were going to die there.

Several years later at a cocktail party, I got into a discussion with a Sherwin-Williams' employee about Sherwin-Williams' recent financial problems and what they were going to do about them. Here was my chance to find out about the company's future plans.

My new friend caused me to shake my head in wonderment when he said, "Boy, that Sherwin-Williams is too high priced now. Sure wish I had bought the stock when it was at $2.50 a share. Look at where I would be now, instead of a salaried employee!"

I asked myself why I hadn't tracked the stock more diligently. At $2.50 a share I would have bought several thousand shares. I would have bought the stock at $3 a share, but why did I miss it dropping so low? This conversation gnawed at me. Especially since the stock was now in the high 30s, or a 15-time increase from a $2.50 share pricing. I had spent so much time tracking the stock for years and now I had missed an opportunity to buy one of the better stocks at a price which was the bargain of the century.

I dismissed the lost opportunity, telling myself the $2–$3 pricing was probably a fluke. It probably happened in one day so I shouldn't feel bad about missing that opportunity. Anybody who tracked it diligently deserved to buy it at $2.50. I didn't track it diligently so I didn't deserve to buy it. End of that story. Or was it just the mere beginning of a more interesting detective novel?

Still, it bothered me. I decided that I would never let that happen to me again. At the library I pulled out the old charts of Sherwin-Williams. Sure enough the most recent chart showed that it had traded as low as $2.50 per share for not one day but *for months!* Did I have my head in the sand at that time? Was I in intensive care, waiting for the plug to be pulled? No, I was fully conscious and aware of what was happening.

Why did I miss the articles, the stories, the reports on the company when it went to an all-time low of $2.50 a share?

Now, I was getting upset. I can miss a one-day buying opportunity and not feel bad. But miss two months of trading in that range? Now that's cause for regret. I could not believe that I had missed the buy of the century! The chances of my getting another buy opportunity like this was nearly impossible.

Figure 17.1 shows the price action of Sherwin-Williams stock from 1977 to 1988, inclusive, or a span of 12 years. Note that the charts are graphed in logarithmic, not arithmetic, scales. If the price of a stock moves from a very low to a very high number, the graph of its price move will look different on different types of scales. The logarithmic charts are plotted to reflect more accurate percentage price changes instead of absolute price changes which arithmetic charts do. I'm not a practitioner of using logarithmic charts since they visually distort my sense of constancy.

The stock moved from a low of $2.50 a share to a high price of $38 per share in 1987. This was a phenomenal increase of over 15 times in a short period of ten years and at an annualized gain of 31.27 percent per year! The stock traded between $2.50–$3.50 per share from 1978 to 1979, inclusive; this was a twenty-four-month period during which I would have been able to buy the stock at such low prices. Or was this the real case?

As I investigated later, this was never the case even though the chart showed that I could have bought it at $2.50! Let's examine the price of Sherwin-Williams from earlier chart books. As I pored over earlier chart books I noticed something strange. Even though the company was the same—Sherwin-Williams—the price patterns of the charts did not look the same. This difference in price shape is evident despite the logarithmic scaling used for prices.

Look at Figures 17.2–17.3. Figure 17.2 shows the price action of the company from 1960–1971 when prices traded between $24 and $80 per share. Figure 17.3 is

FIGURE 17.1 Sherwin-Williams: 1977–1989

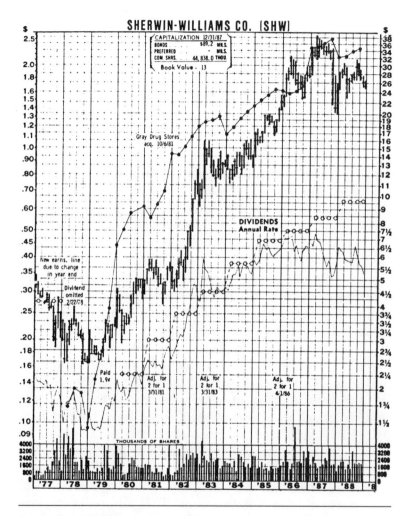

FIGURE 17.2 Sherwin-Williams: 1960–1971

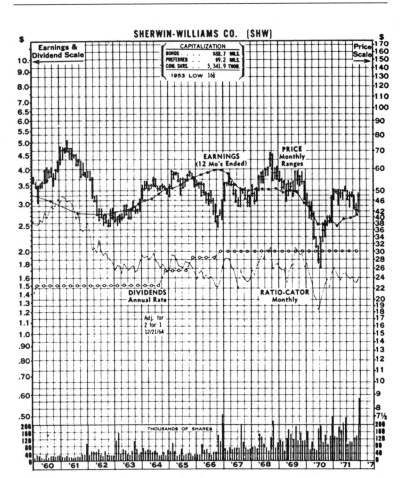

Source: Reprinted by permission of Securities Research Company

the same stock, but with a time range from 1971 to 1983. I intentionally picked the two charts out for you to compare the price pattern. The reader would expect Figure 17.2 to line up exactly with Figure 17.3 since Figure 17.2 ended with 1971 and Figure 17.3 started with 1971. Surprisingly, the two charts just won't match up! The

---

FIGURE 17.3 Sherwin-Williams: 1971–1983

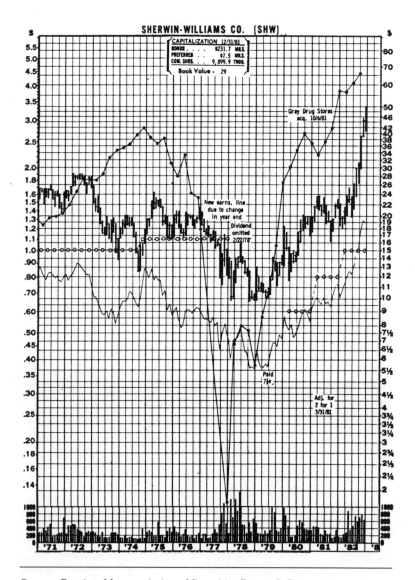

Source: Reprinted by permission of Securities Research Company

chart pattern for Figure 17.2 showed a price range from
$7 to $65 a share and ended with the stock priced out at
about $46 a share at the end of 1971. Figure 17.3
started with the stock priced out at about $24 a share at
the beginning of 1971.

I've tracked the same company from 1960 to 1989 by
showing the reader three different charts, and not a single
one shows similar price patterns. In fact, none of the three
even shows the same highs and lows. What happened?

The answer is stock splits. Now, let's list the dates
and type of stock splits for Sherwin-Williams from 1960
to 1988.

12/21/64	2 for 1
03/31/81	2 for 1
03/31/83	2 for 1
04/01/86	2 for 1

From 1960 to 1988, there were four stock splits.
There was one lonely stock split on 12/21/64. Then for
the next 17 years there were no stock splits until
03/31/81. This stock split was promptly followed by the
last two—one only two years later, and the fourth three
years after that one. The last three stocks splits
occurred within a span of six years! The company management had maximized the stock split to their best
advantage!

Let's follow the course of this stock split history. If
you had owned one share of the company's stock prior to
12/21/64 (approximately since there is a previous date
that you must be an owner of record of the stock prior to
the actual split date; often this "owner of record" date is
several weeks prior to the actual split date), you would
now have two shares on 12/21/64, four shares on
03/31/81, eight shares on 03/31/83, and 16 shares on
04/01/86 of the company. So for this period, from one
share of old stock, you now have 16 new shares of the

company! I look at this and say that I should forget about the price. Just taking a look at the "return" on number of shares from the original one share, I've got a 1600 percent increase from 1964 to 1986. Annualized that's 26 percent per year on the number of shares alone!

The next set of charts will help the reader see what happened to the stock between Figures 17.2 and 17.3.

Figure	Price Activity
17.4	1961–1972
17.5	1962–1973
17.6	1963–1974
17.6	1964–1975

Compare the patterns in Figures 17.4 and 17.10. Figure 17.4 shows the 12/21/64 stock split. Figures 17.5 and 17.9 show no stock splits and the price patterns of all these separate charts are similar in appearance. Figure 17.10 shows the second stock split and now, because the stock has split, all previous prices have to be readjusted to reflect a two-for-one stock split! In Figure 17.10, the 2-for-1 stock split on 03/31/81 forces that particular chart to be redrawn at half of what the previous scale had been. Take the lows and highs that glare out at you in all the charts prior to Figure 17.10: $26 low in middle 1970 (Figure 17.4); $25 low at the end of 1974 (Figure 17.6); $20 low at the beginning and end of 1978 (Figure 17.8); and the high of about $56 in mid-1972 (Figure 17.6). Note that in all the charts they are constant and you know that the highs and lows were at those dollars.

Let's jump to Figure 17.10 which has now been created after the second 2-for-1 stock split of 03/31/81. If

FIGURE 17.4 Sherwin-Williams: 1961–1973

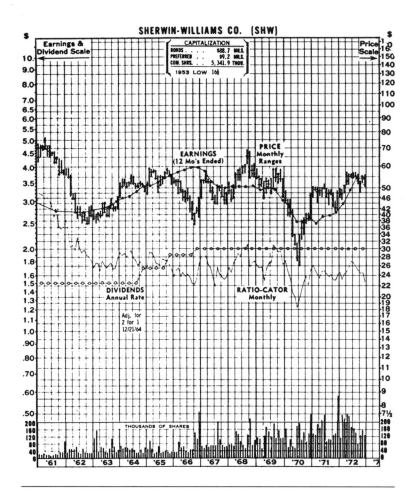

Source: Reprinted by permission of Securities Research Company

FIGURE 17.5 Sherwin-Williams: 1962–1974

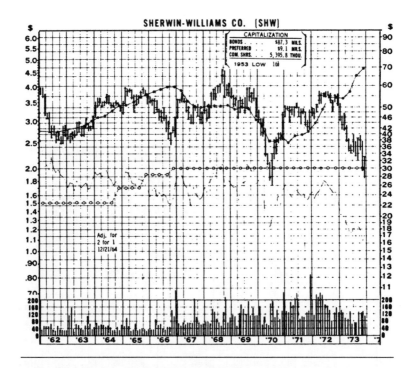

Source: Reprinted by permission of Securities Research Company

you were to look for the lows of $20, $25, $26 or the high of $56, you would never find them in that chart! Why? Because all the prices have been adjusted by half to reflect the stock split. Your previous low of $20 has now become $10, the $25 has become $12.50, the $26 has become $13, and the high has become $28! And because of the 16-for-one split for this time period of analysis, the $10 low of Figure 17.8 for the early and end of 1978, has now become $2.50 a share; the $5 for the early and end of 1978 prior to the 03/31/83 split has

FIGURE 17.6 Sherwin-Williams: 1963–1975

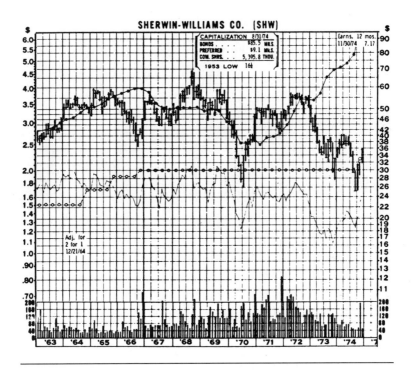

Source: Reprinted by permission of Securities Research Company

now become $2.50 a share, and so forth. Confusing? You bet!

Of course, the solution to this obvious attempt at rewriting history, is to take the number of stock splits listed and work your way back. Honestly, though, how many of us diligent investors would actually go through the process of doing this? This example was a very clean example since it only involved rewriting history with the use of simple ratio stock splits! Some companies complicate the rewriting process by using different split ratios.

FIGURE 17.7 Sherwin-Williams: 1964–1976

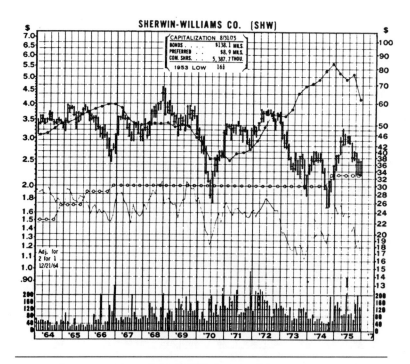

Source: Reprinted by permission of Securities Research Company

FIGURE 17.8 Sherwin-Williams: 1968–1979

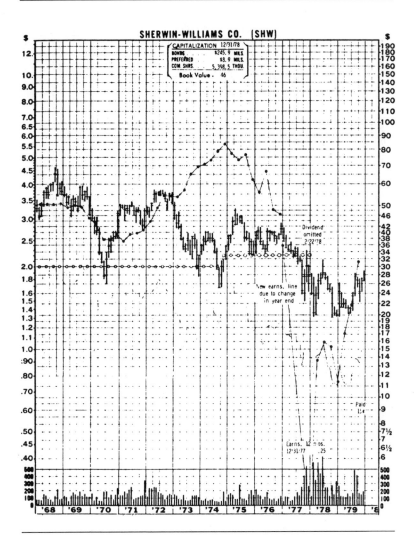

Source: Reprinted by permission of Securities Research Company

FIGURE 17.9 Sherwin-Williams: 1969–1980

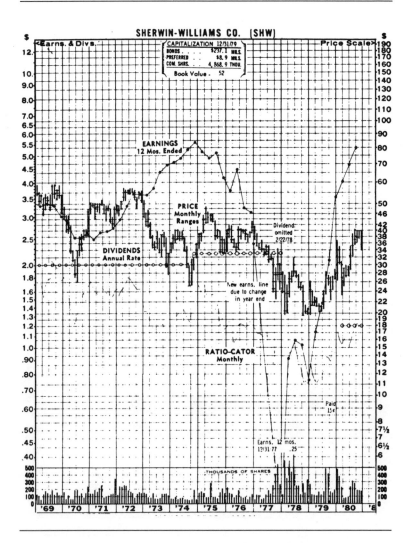

Source: Reprinted by permission of Securities Research Company

102

FIGURE 17.10 Sherwin-Williams: 1970–1981

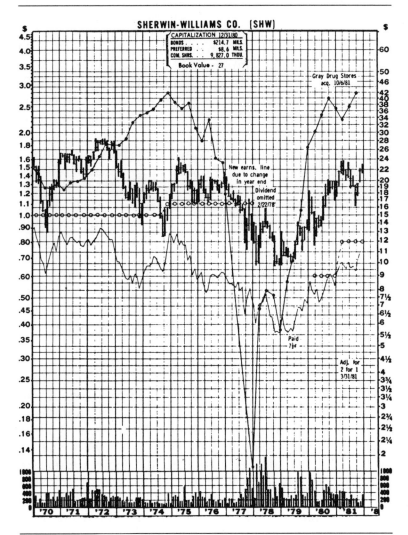

Source: Reprinted by permission of Securities Research Company

If you had a hard time working the thread of this chapter, you'll never get through the task of reworking ratio splits!

From an analyst's point of view, what are some of the ramifications? Well, the obvious one is that one could never have bought 100 shares of the stock at $2.50 a share to see it rise meteorically to $35 a share! The best anyone could have done was to have bought 1/16 of 100 shares at $20 a share in 1978, where the splits adjusted low of $2.50 a share was made. This meant you couldn't have plowed $10,000 into buying 4,000 shares at $2.50 in 1978, but could only buy $10,000 of 500 shares of stock trading at $20 a share. These are two entirely different sets of mindsets from two sets of different investors. At $2.50, I'll take a flyer on such a good company. At $20 a share, I'm less aggressive on buying the stock.

Another ramification is that the high of about $75 made on the old figure (Figure 17.2) is more intimidating than the "high" of $38 in the new figure (Figure 17.1). Numerically $38 is a good price to pay for a solid company, but at $75 the price is a bit rich, even for solid companies. Both prices are from the same company! Marketing is even critical in stocks and the experts are very sensitive to this.

The Sherwin-Williams figures show you that if you had a current figure of the stock with itemized dates of what and when the stock splits occurred, you could go backward and recalculate the actual lows made in actual time. By looking at the current figures after the many stock splits the lows and highs are all adjusted highs and lows, not actual *tradeable* lows or highs.

As complex as this example of Sherwin-Williams is to the novice investor, it is simple to readjust. Some stocks are not only split, but also adjusted for stock dividends. Can you imagine the difficulty of readjusting the actual highs and lows by recalculating values based on stock splits AND stock issued dividends?

Stock splits and stock dividends are the mechanics of the marketplace to hide and rewrite the past to the detriment of the current investors and the benefit of the issuing companies! And I thought they just wanted my money so they could give me an opportunity to share in the growth of the United States . . .

With idle time comes introspection. I wonder what a reverse stock split does?

RULE 18

Behind the Obvious Success of One Trader Lie the Invisible Failures of a Hundred Traders

This is evident in life and most acutely in the markets. If you are to move from the markets to real life and expect the ratios and the results of winners to losers to be different, then you will be sadly disappointed.

We were sitting around one day commiserating the miserable fact that most of the deals I had created since I left the trading floor environment had turned sour. Frankly, I had a limit to my largesse in funding these deals also.

Since I had retired from the floor trading environment, I had to relearn and rethink what it was that I needed to do. I had heard horror stories of fellow traders who left the business or invested their profits from trading into other businesses. Inordinately, they all lost their money.

I had stashed some money away when I cashed out my chips and decided to start up several businesses. One person would come to me with an idea, and I would say that sounded good. Then I asked how much he needed. Fine I would say and then I would fund the operation. This happened for several years.

What was interesting, and at this time amusing, about all this was inevitably these people would always come back to me for more money. Without a doubt they didn't need my time, nor my expertise, but merely my money. I had found another role for myself: Sugar Daddy to the idiots of the world.

Wanting my money was fine with me since it was the only thing I had that was of any value to these projects.

After a string of losses in failed projects I sat back and wondered what was wrong with these deals. After thoroughly analyzing them, I came to the conclusion that fault rested in a myriad of places. One common denominator was that all these deals involved me. I couldn't believe that I was the common cause of why these projects failed, especially when I didn't manage the people, didn't work with them on a daily basis, didn't cut the checks to pay the expenses, etc.

As I later discovered, I failed because I merely "didn't . . . " Let me explain.

I couldn't fathom why the common denominator, me, could be the cause of the failures.

It was fair. It was my money. It was my choice to invest. I wasn't throwing someone else's money down the drain. Yet, my hard-earned money was. Sometimes slowly, sometimes with such a force that the backflush was enough to drag me into the drain, too.

After one too many of these incidences I found myself in the spiraling drain. Probably for the last time I thought back then. A revelation occurred to me right then and there! It was as if the god of bad trades whacked me on the side of my head and had awakened me. It's surprising, isn't it, to find astounding eye-opening revelations when you are on the verge of total and complete annihilation?

What I discovered was that while I was at the core of the monetary losses, it wasn't my actions that caused the losses. It was because of my inaction that these losses occurred. It was really the acts of "didn'ts" that caused my losses.

Instead of dealing with the markets I was dealing with people. Normal, human, everyday people. The answer to why I was failing in coming to the same amount of success in business investments that I had had in the trading and investment worlds rested with the difference between dealing with the markets and dealing with people.

In the markets I controlled my risks, my markets to play, my position exposure, and my equity exposure. I spent hours in researching markets to play. I watched and observed the markets I wanted to trade before I made the speculation or investment. The interaction was between me and the markets. I controlled my activity and I managed the markets.

It was entirely different with business deals. In business deals I saw many ideas when people came to me. I liked some of the ideas and discarded the others. I spent a lot of time in discussing the validity of these ideas with others. I researched the ideas for many hours. Once I decided the ideas were good, I invested my money with the people who came to me with these ideas. Then I left the scene, expecting the people to bring these concepts to fruition.

What an assumption for me to expect people to execute.

Though I was able to control myself, I gave my money away. I did not manage the people. So my money went down the tubes.

At the same time I embarked on a mission to write specialized books to help people succeed in the markets. This, as I was later introspectively able to discern, was the "control group action." This control group action which concurrently existed at the time of the miserable failures in making deals pointed out something which was not obvious to me at first. The first book is in its seventh printing. The second one is in its fifth printing. The third is selling well and fourth book just went into its third printing. You are reading my fifth book. People in the publishing business are amazed that my books have done so well. This success is based on a condition similar to my success as a trader: I depended on myself.

Trading is a loner's profession. Writing is one, too. By accident I gravitated toward a profession I could easily duplicate both in environment and dependencies. By accident, the writing was the control group action which I later compared to my investment projects!

Investing in businesses run by others is not a loner's profession. Instead of treating these investments as needing lots and lots of management skills, I treated them as concepts which merely needed investment capital. I saw the ideas. I liked the ideas. I invested my money and walked away. At least, I tried to walk away.

How many times have you invested money in limited partnerships, packaged deals, where you merely expected a check at the end of the quarter and were thoroughly disappointed? The checks came, but with an attached memo: "Due to circumstances beyond our control expenses more than doubled. . . . Our company president embezzled more money than we thought. . . . Our founder died in an airplane crash. . . . " More often than you would like to remember? You manage your career well but entrust others to do your thinking and handling of your own hard earned cash? How stupid and silly.

The amount of freedom from management of the people I entrusted my money to was entirely proportional to the amount of money I lost: the more freedom I gave people to run their own companies, the more money I lost. It started to turn into an axiom—an uncontestable, immutable law of nature.

But why could people not come through with their end? As an optimist I couldn't conclude that people are failures. If I were to accept this conclusion then a host of other problems would have to be dealt with, such as:

1. Could or should I continue to work with others? And if I do, should I lower my expectations of colleagues?
2. Can people be trusted to come through with their end? And if not, whom could I trust in the business world?
3. Would I be better off finding projects that I could handle by myself? Or, do I push my own sets of skills and talents beyond their levels of effectiveness to accomplish tasks that would normally require cooperation with others?

Below are my other conclusions, which may also help you:

1. **If you come from an entirely different area of life than those people coming to you for capital, beware.** When an "outsider" such as you are asked for investment capital, the money seekers have already exhausted the sources within the industry. If people within the industry who purportedly know more about the business than you do don't want to put up the money, then why should you? If you're an auto mechanic and someone comes to you looking for capital to open up a restaurant, forget it. If someone comes to you looking for capital to open up an auto dealership, then you're in better shape. There are stellar successes where "outsiders" do make a bundle, but as a general rule you will be subject to losses you have no control over.
2. **The success/failure ratios in all professions are similar.** A person who is successful in trading

110

will be successful elsewhere. It might take a little more time to get up to speed in the learning curve department. A person who is a failure in one field is most likely to be a failure in another field. As pejorative as this conclusion is, the implication is that there are general success traits found in successful people which cross all fields. You can hone these traits and skills for yourself by reading some of the self-help books currently available.

3. **If you are going to invest your money outside of your area(s) of knowledge, you must watch, manage and guide the people who will be playing with your money**. You mustn't do what most investors do: relinquish control of the money and literally pray for a return of capital. Everything has a cost. Even simple returns from investing in money market funds. The rate of return is relatively low because somebody had to be paid for their time and efforts to get you the return, as piddling as the amount is.

From my own experience, a counterpoint from these conclusions exists. I've seen people who have succeeded in their business or professional careers and come into the markets only to lose all their hard-earned money. Here, the problem is that they are taking their experience of managing and attempting to hold tight the course of their ships' movements. Try as they will they cannot do this in the markets. In the markets they must have faith a trend will continue, losses will mount if not cut, profits will accumulate if allowed to, reversals do not happen in one day, etc. They must learn there is greater emphasis on doing all the preliminary research before the positions are entered. In the real world from which they are coming, the emphasis is on handholding and guiding the management and employees to a final outcome. Make these two distinctions, treat them in the appropriate manner, and you will find more than ample success in both arenas.

People who do succeed in life will find success in other areas, but finding others who have experienced a similar level of success will become progressively harder as they continue onwards to their success comfort zone. This is a natural law. How many people can be at the head of the class? Only one. How many people can be world class athletes? Only a handful. How many can be superb traders? Only a few that I know of.

In the arcane world of trading there are many who envy the successes of the few stellar traders. The successes of these traders are justifiably deserved. Similarly the failures of the hundreds of traders are reflections that not everyone can get to the top.

In life, know that behind the few visibly successful people are the less visible hundreds who have not achieved the same levels of success. So, treasure the few who do succeed and never disparage those who have tried but have not succeeded.

RULE 19

A Broker Who Can Make Money for You Deserves Not Only Lunch but Dinner from You

One of the few advantages of getting older is that your friends of the same age group and ilk are inheriting assets.

A friend who recently inherited several million dollars said to me that he disliked brokers immensely. Since he had invited me to dinner and I didn't want to pick up the tab I listened, rather inattentively, however. I know now how women feel when they go out on first dates with uninteresting men. He went on to say that his broker had made $30,000 last year in net commissions on my friend's stock trading account. My friend, when I asked him, said that his trading account only netted him $20,000 in profits after a year of activity. He was outraged that his broker made more money than he did!

It was a good thing I wasn't swallowing a bite of my dinner at the time my friend drummed on the dinner table. Otherwise, he would have had to perform the

Heimlich maneuver on me to force the errant food morsels out of the clogged esophagus.

My friend went on and on. He pointed out each stock play his broker had gotten him into and the amount of money that he made or lost. He went on and on.

After this relentless badmouthing of his broker I said to my friend, "Since when is it written in stone that a broker is obligated to make money for you?" Dumb silence. Now, dear reader, I've never met my friend's broker and as far as I'm concerned I really don't need to so I'm not defending him because of a friendship.

I continued by saying that a broker makes money for himself regardless of whether or not he is making money for his clients! It so happened that my friend found a broker who knew what he was doing for the client and made money for the client, too. So, my friend was going to chew out his broker because the broker made more money than my friend did? Give the man a break. He did his job well and performed better than a vast majority of the brokers out there, whose only obligations to clients are to get good executions and maintain good account records.

My friend's attitude about brokers was very disparaging. I know brokers; even those who perform with the due diligence of a Soros-Templeton pairing would become disillusioned after dealing with the public.

After dinner, my friend lightened up and said that taking his broker to lunch wasn't the thing to do, but dinner was certainly in order!

Brokers deserve recognition for jobs well done. But not all deserve recognition. In 1993, the stock market went straight up. The public who came into the market at that time caught the last upward move in stocks. Practically any buy recommendation by anyone, rookie brokers included, resulted in profitable trading. My caveat to brokers is that they mustn't allow the results of the last bull move to indicate to them they are good stock pickers. And investors shouldn't necessarily bestow brokers with above-average market acumen when this particular stock trend obviously made dartboard stock selection the sweetheart of Wall Street analysis. Nevertheless, rewards should be shown to brokers who do well for their clients. Rewards aren't based only on commissions for the brokers will get that regardless of whether you, the client, makes or loses money. Instead, you could base the rewards on how the broker treats you as an account to be valued for years to come.

RULE 20

Never Break a Sound Rule (If You Feel You Are Breaking One, Reduce Your Commitment)

Now, this rule is an excellent example of nebulous thinking. What is a sound rule? That's so nebulous. In fact what is an unsound rule? I've often wondered why I would knowingly break a rule if I knew it were sound.

This is essentially the paradox I learned a long time ago. The concept of soundness is so relative. What I found to be sound was unsound to someone else. What someone else found to be sound I laughed at disdainfully and said that I never considered *that* rule to be problematic, or more appropriately, unsound!

In a simplistic fashion, sound is whatever you deem the rule to be. If the rules are sound to begin with, you will find that your breaking the rules will indicate you should never have broken them in the first place! This tautology appears to be circular, which in a sense, is true. Yet, there is no other way around this, no pun intended.

This concept of trying to figure out the definition of soundness is the enigma. I never had a problem with

116

shorting stocks or commodities. My reasoning was that markets go up and they go down. It would be silly not to short the market to make money on the downside. Others have a hard time figuring out that the markets also go down, so they never short the markets. I used to have a problem with overtrading. Some others I know never go beyond one lots. Others can say to me they like to track all markets. I have a problem tracking more than the numbers that can be counted on the fingers of both my hands.

Who's to say that one is right and the other is wrong?

The only way you can determine whether or not the rule you are considering is sound or not is to test the rule out for yourself. You must go through the learning process for yourself. You must test the rule against your own parameters, whatever they may be. In the process of testing and violating these sound rules, you will also learn more about your mental makeup and know your strengths and weaknesses.

In a similar manner, once you find out what "sound" means to you, you will be less inclined to break these rules because you will have had the experience of working with them. With this experience comes the confidence that to follow the rule is to insure success. You will know that to break the rule will guarantee eventual losses.

Once I had established what I considered to be sound rules for my own trading, I tested them. In fact, they continually undergo testing because the markets are always in flux. (One condition always exists in these tests: I never allow any one test to put me into financial ruin!)

I have had occasions to take a sound trading or investment rule and change it ever so slightly. If you asked me why I would do a dumb thing like this, I can only reply it seemed okay at the time.

When I broke sound trading rules, either I did not fully understand the rule, or I knew the rule well enough that I could play around with it (I feel very uncomfortable in doing this, however).

I would give more credibility to the first reason when I started my trading career—I didn't know what the rule entailed. So it was not uncommon for me to add to losers, buy on the highs, sell on the lows, spread myself too thin, trade many more contracts than I could handle comfortably, and a myriad of other actions.

As I gained more experience in the markets I would change the rule or break it because I knew what the rule was effectively used for and would be able to sidestep the expected results if I broke the rule.

Even after all the experience I had garnered in the markets I found breaking these rules stressful and taxing to do. The deliberate violations of these sound rules caused me to be mentally upset because lurking in the back of my mind was the absolute truth, fact, and reality; I would lose money if I continued breaking these sound rules.

I learned that I could avoid the stress by strictly adhering to the rules. Simple solution to a simple problem. If you don't want to go to jail, don't do anything that can get you in jail. Absolutely.

The benefits, efficiency or profits to be gained by violating the sound rules are marginal, at best. What I mean by marginal is not that one trade in which you violate a rule and make a lot of money; this type of trade is marginal not because the profits are huge, but the spirit of garnering those profits is marginal. The chances of making those huge profits by violating the rule again in the future is slim; to the contrary, violating the rule may again create a lot of small losses or one huge loss.

It's like jaywalking on the German Autobahn. The many times you are able to violate the rule you can safely cross the road; the one time that you violate the rule but get hit by a speeding car is the catastrophic moment.

There's also an element of comfort in knowing that if you follow the rules you can expect a certain outcome. Deviation from the rule warrants punishment through losses. No other way around this.

RULE 21

Never Overtrade;
Trading Correctly Is
More Important
Than You Think

This chapter is about an insidious problem that traders must be aware of and avoid: overtrading. The use of derivatives has increased this problem. As we trade globally and geographic borders between nations give way to electronic superhighways, the problems of overtrading will persist and magnify.

Trading the markets correctly has always been very important. In our age of globalized finances, it becomes critical. One company president can take down a company over time with bad management decisions; one company treasurer with trading responsibilities can take down a company with one bad telephone call. If we are not careful, a federal treasurer can cause a government to collapse.

Disarming Disinterest Pervasive in the Management Community

In 1989, as I embarked upon my career as a financial writer, I submitted an outline for an article on the problems that companies face when dealing with traders in their corporate treasury departments. I sent my proposal to the premier business management magazine in the world, *Harvard Business Review*. In my cover letter I suggested the possibility that one person in a corporation could take down the whole company, a company which was created by the sweat and effort of thousands of employees over the span of several generations. This singular person was identified as a trader in the treasury department of these companies, who with one single phone call could literally wipe out the existence of the company! The magazine turned down my article. In brief they indicated their subscribing managers would not have any interest.

However, the need for this kind of article has not diminished. With attitudes such as those proffered by such a mainstream magazine, it comes as no surprise that some corporate management has allowed individual traders in corporate treasury departments to run amuck. I'd like to warn the treasurers that we have yet to see the worst of the financial derivatives debacle. Brace yourselves for a global collapse simply as a result of human nature. I've seen traders destroy themselves because they didn't know how to trade. Now, we're seeing corporate treasurers-turned-traders take tremendous risks unknowingly because they don't know how to trade.

My background is self-taught as a trader for my own account. From first hand experience, as member of several stocks, options and futures, exchanges, I saw a lot of traders take it on the chin when their positions went awry after market conditions went abruptly against them. In 1973, we saw the development of the first centralized stock options exchange, the Chicago Board of Options Exchange. Since then we have seen explosive growth in options trading.

As a trader I learned the hard way to discipline myself mentally from taking extraordinarily large positions with my limited capital. I learned *never to overtrade,* regardless of what I was trading: stocks, futures, or options. If you overtrade and lose, this is for keeps.

Derivatives Debacle Trilogy: Part I

I retired from active floor trading for my own account in 1986 to set up my writing career. From the sidelines I watched the unfolding of Part I of the first derivatives debacle of the trilogy, which the floor traders at the Chicago Board Options Exchange faced in 1987. During the crash of 1987 when the Dow Jones Industrial Average dropped over 500 points, instead of proving to be a benefit, derivatives became the bane of some options traders' existence!

Overnight, previous option positions, which had neither long nor short market biases, exploded to infinite "long-sided" positions in a collapsing market.

That's the beauty and danger of leverage. With a lot of positions, the leverage can magnify geometrically when the underlying moves only fractionally. In the case of the dropping market, the underlying moved a lot, and the derivatives positions moved enough to bulge eyeballs, throb hearts, and twist larger intestines. A few of my trader friends were carted off the exchange floor that day never to be heard from or seen again.

Shortly after the meltdown week, I saw future problems that could develop with indiscriminate use of leveraged trading products. And these products were foisted on naive and inexperienced treasurers who became traders overnight. But the mantle of trader is not a title handed over to an employee along with the raise. It must be treated with greater respect. "Trader" must be earned through trial and error but without too much risk.

Some of these individual traders have created their own little fiefdoms, protecting and sheltering their roles and their departments with arcane terminology (forwards, straddles, rollovers, etc.) and even more obtuse strategies (delta neutral spreads, backspreads, iron butterflies, jelly rolls, etc.). In the late 1980s and the early 1990s, corporate management did not pay heed to the "whole heap of trouble" some of these traders were getting the other "9,999" employees into.

Being long a million shares isn't bad when the stock goes up. Being long one share is horrible when the stock goes down. The principle in both cases is the same: when you're right, you are right; when you are wrong, being committed to only a miniscule position is still absolutely wrong! This is all part of trading correctly.

Similarly, when 9,999 employees work hard to build up a company, that's excellent management; when all 9,999 employees go on strike, that's terrible management. When one employee goes awry, even though the rest are doing their jobs perfectly well, management is still at fault.

Part II

Although the magazine rejected the article because they considered the scope of the topic too narrow for their audience, I'm sure this topic is now interesting to their readers since we have just witnessed Part Two of the derivatives debacle.

The former treasurer of Orange County in California did what no successful trader should ever do: He lost sight of what his role was.

A man with such a position of control over so many assets, which did not personally belong to him, took a shot and lost a lot!

He lost between $1.7 to $2 billion dollars, in a few short months, of the assets over which he had fiduciary responsibilities.

Recently, a single trader at Baring Securities of London managed to lose over $1.4 billion of the investment banker's money in less than two months' time, thus putting four thousand employees' jobs at risk. Ironically this trader did use good equity management. His $1.4 billion loss was derived from positions worth about $28 billion. That's only a mere 5 percent that the trader lost of the total positions. The 5 percent is within acceptable exposure parameters. Kudos to his skill at managing his equity exposure. Unfortunately, he used the leverage available with the futures contracts he traded. Using a presumed, and conservative, leverage of 10 percent cash controlling the other 90 percent of the futures contracts value, he multiplied his trading capital 10-fold to 50 times! With multipliers as large as this one, it doesn't take much movement to get this trader and his position into deep trouble.

These two examples involved considerably more position risk, not necessarily more money, than a simple trader's account at the options exchange. I'm sure anybody in his most insane moment would not risk $5,000,000 in derivatives positions when he had only $100,000 in his trading account; but this very same person could unknowingly be longer and longer in a rapidly declining market based on his assumption, albeit wrong, of position risks. This is exactly how each of these traders exposed their assets: they were oblivious to position risk. In a sense, they overtraded without knowing it.

The second part of this trilogy involved off-exchange traded products which banks and brokerage companies created and sold, well away from the jurisdiction of the options exchanges' SEC-controlled environment! But these very same people in these banks and brokerage companies say that they don't want SEC or other government controls.

We all believe in the invisible hand guiding the markets. In the context of global markets and Darwinian survival one could argue that Orange County deserved to perish. Orange County and her managers couldn't take the pressures so why should they exist? Who are these bankers and brokers kidding when they advocate this position? Give these clients the toy gun and expect them to stop at using caps? Most will, but a few others will move on to play with dangerous armaments. I don't worry about guys who stop at cap guns; I worry about those who drag us into global financial wars. And we are quickly approaching financial global warring.

The bankers and brokers are not going to take the responsibility of educating these clients on position risks. Witness how Merrill Lynch claimed their agency role in Citron's Orange County fiasco. However weak their argument, bankers' and brokers' defenses have always been based on their role of "agency." As agents of the corporations they aren't culpable for the products and services they have sold.

The second part of this trilogy has shown us only the tip of the iceberg. Someone must protect these traders and corporations from themselves, and secondly, prevent them from inflicting financial risk and harm to trusting beneficiaries. The solution: Bring in government controls, reporting functions, and risk controls. I may be accused of limiting the free market arm in trading, but I won't be faulted for allowing individual traders who have no idea of the difficulty of trading correctly to take down whole companies. The game is no longer a simple buy or sell decision. The amount of financial power in the hands of the few have increased tremendously over the last few years of financial warring.

Part III

Implied in this call for stricter government control of the financial arena is the assumption some of these singular traders don't always know what they're doing. You're absolutely right in concluding that. Everybody can make money when the economy is booming. We don't hire these managers to do that in boom times: We hire them to cover our liability risks. If they want to speculate, they speculate on their own time and with their own money. They mustn't and cannot speculate with other people's money for which they have fiduciary responsibilities.

We now have two data points to help us plot the direction of international financial stress. The first was the 1987 stock options debacle at the beginning, with options traded on the Chicago Board Options Exchange. The second data point is the ongoing debacle in the derivatives markets. Municipalities with billions under control of their treasurers are suffering greatly because of their treasurers' inability to trade the markets safely. I'm not talking about trading markets well for that requires years of trading experience. I'm merely talking about trading safely with a very keen eye toward position risks.

There are no controls imposed by these singular traders on themselves to limit position risks.

With two datapoints already in place we can draw a line. The trend line slopes toward larger and more stressful financial disasters in the trading areas. The individual exchange members got whacked. The corporate treasurers are getting their fill right now.

Where is the third data point to be found; where will the next derivatives debacle occur? This point has to be larger than exchange traders and corporate treasurers combined!

What are the largest entities? Governments. Large-scale, manmade institutions controlling the assets of millions of their constituents. Some in these governments do not know what position risks are. As an experienced trader, I know exactly my position risks when I initiate positions. Unfortunately, this experience came painfully slow. Government employees can take down a

FIGURE 21.1 Cover letter

Financial Options Consultants

SPECIALIZED
FINANCIAL
CONSULTANTS

780 SO. FEDERAL   SUITE #314
CHICAGO, ILLINOIS 60605
(312) 663-9339

February 27, 1989

Mr. Alan M. Webber
Managing Editor
Harvard Business Review
Boston, MA 02163

Dear Mr. Webber:

I spoke to you on February 15, 1989 concerning an idea for an article in the Harvard Business Review about the management of a trader's daily role within a corporation's treasury.

The article, tentatively titled "Managing the Trader," will discuss the role of a trader who is a risk manager for his corporation. Information on discovering where and how the trader can usurp his legitimate role for his own aggrandizement will be examined.   This article details how the trader can expose his corporation to unlimited losses if his market analysis is wrong and at the same time how he can benefit if his gamble pays off.   The article will define what the role of a trader is, how well he performs this role, how he can usurp this role for his own benefit, how to hire, fire and compensate traders, and what the future of computer-aided trading will mean to the corporate manager.

I've enclosed several articles in various business publications which detailed how traders have exposed their employers to unlimited risk while allowing themselves unlimited professional and monetary rewards.   An outline of the proposed article is enclosed.   Articles I have written and reviews of my first book are also enclosed for your reference.

If you believe your readers can benefit from this article I would like to discuss this idea with you.   As the world trading community heads toward a centralized, electronic forum, the role of traders as risk managers becomes critical.   Upper corporate managers can waste the assets of corporations through bad management decisions; traders can destroy with one telephone call.

Sincerely,

William F. Eng
Founder and Consultant

enc.

cc file

127

FIGURE 21.1 Cover letter (continued)

```
     Outline for "Managing the Trader" by William F. Eng

I.   Trader's Role in Corporate Asset Risk Management

     A.   Risk Hedging Manager
     B.   Market Speculation
     C.   Special Case:  The Liar

  II. Profits and Losses from Traders

     A.   Alacrity of Losses
     B.   Globalization of Losses
     C.   Types of Accounts
          1.  Trader's Accounts
               a.   Personal Trading Accounts
               b.   Corporate Trading Accounts
          2.  Concealed Accounts
               a.   Discovery
               b.   Tracing
               c.   Limiting

III.How to Limit Corporate Exposure

     A.   Tracking Order Execution
     B.   Tell-tale Signs of Illegal Dealings
     C.   Compensation Scales
     D.   "When Issued" Problems
     E.   Peer Group Enforcements
     F.   Personnel Management Policies
          1.  Hiring
          2.  Firing
          3.  Compensation
     G.   Order Processing
          1. Centralized
          2. End of Day Checking
     H.   Daytrading -- risks of non accountability

IV.  Future Problems
     A.   Computer-Aided Trading (CAT)
     B.   "Electronification" of Markets
     C.   Fungibility of Contracts
     D.   Computer Programmer Thievery

 V. Conclusions
```

---

government operation if they have not learned the patience of trading well.

Brace yourselves. This last derivative debacle will be one big one. In the interim, hone your trading skills. It will be the one time in history where government disgorges revenues to their constituents.

FIGURE 21.2 Rejection letter

HARVARD UNIVERSITY

GRADUATE SCHOOL OF BUSINESS ADMINISTRATION

GEORGE F. BAKER FOUNDATION

HARVARD BUSINESS REVIEW

MAIL ADDRESS:
HARVARD BUSINESS REVIEW
BOSTON, MASSACHUSETTS 02163

617-495-
FAX: 617-495-9933
TELEX: 6817320

March 31, 1989

Mr. William F. Eng
780 South Federal Street
Suite 314
Chicago, Illinois 60605

Dear Mr. Eng:

Thank you for submitting your manuscript, "Managing the Trader."
The editors have reviewed it, and I am sorry to report that we
will be unable to accept it for publication in the <u>Harvard
Business Review</u>.

Your manuscript addresses an interesting topic. However, it is
not a topic which we think is of immediate or urgent concern to
most of our readers. <u>HBR</u> readers are by and large practicing
executives who look to our magazine for practical insights and
guidelines that make them more effective in their jobs.
Successful <u>HBR</u> articles blend original and thought provoking
analysis with telling examples and cases.

We do appreciate your thinking of us. Good luck placing your
manuscript elsewhere.

Sincerely,

William Taylor

RULE 22

All Numeric Relations Lead to 0.618

Much has been written about summation series. The waning popularity of the Fibonacci summation series has been give life again by several recently published books. (See *The Best Stocks to Trade for 1995* for more details.)

Several years ago while I was writing my first book, I made a thorough study of the Fibonacci Summation Series and other summation series that had similar concepts.

Fibonacci Summation Series

The Fibonacci Summation Series is a series of numbers derived by performing a mathematical operation on a previous number. In this mathematical operation, you simply add the current number to the previous number to create a third number. The numbers are related to each other by varying ratios.

Let's take a look at how the Fibonacci Summation Series is derived. The Series is as follows:

1, 1, 2, 3, 5, 8, 13, 21, 34, 55, 89, 144, 233, ad infinitum

We start the summation series with the number 1. To this we add itself to obtain the next number in the series which is 2. To the 2 we add the previous number, 1, to arrive at the next number in the sequence, 3. To the 3 we add the previous number, 2, to arrive at the next number of the sequence, 5. Let's skip to the number 144. If we performed the same addition mathematics, we would then add the previous number to 144, which is 89, to 144 to arrive at the next number in the sequence, 233.

For whatever other possible reasons, the numbers in this summation series are related to each other by varying ratios. If we now took each consecutive number and perform a ratio analysis between any such two sets of numbers we obtain ratios. For example, if we took the pair 3 & 5, which are adjoining each other in the sequence, and divided the former number by the latter, we arrive at a ratio which so happens to be 0.60. If we continue to divide two consecutive numbers of the summation series we will obtain a ratio which is constant, 0.618.

Fibonacci Summation Series Number	Ratio of Number to Previous Number in Sequence
1	not applicable
1	1.000
2	0.500
3	0.66666666 (repeating)
5	0.60000000
8	0.625
13	0.6153846
21	0.6190476
34	0.6176470
55	0.6181818 (repeating)
89	0.6179775
144	0.6180555
233	0.6180257
ad infinitum	not ad infinitum but approaching 0.618

So you can easily see that the 0.618 (rounded off) is pretty well ensconced after the 7th or 8th number in the sequence.

Now Comes the Lucas Summation Series

With the concept of additive numbers to create a summation series, many years ago a mathematician, Eduoard Lucas, created the Lucas Summation Series.

Instead of starting out with the number 1 like the Fibonacci Summation Series, Lucas started out with the numbers 1 and 3. The Lucas Summation Series then became:

1, 3, 4, 7, 11, 18, 29, 47, 76, 123, 199, 322, ad infinitum

If you performed the same ratio analysis we did for the Fibonacci Summation Series you also arrive at the number 0.618. Note that the numbers used both by Fibonacci and Lucas are simple integers with low values.

The Eng Summation Series

As a trader I like to think in BIG numbers. So it was natural for me, who had more time than brains, to fiddle around with other numbers for the summation series.

I happened to discover that the ratio, 0.168, or any such derived related ratio (0.382, 1.618, 1.382, etc.), can be extracted from other sets of two starting numbers. I did not have to be fixed on how the summation series started. All I had to do was add the first two numbers I chose. The resultant summation series then would have properties similar to the Fibonacci and Lucas summations series. I had discovered a summation series on which the Fibonacci and Lucas summation series were subsets!

For disbelievers I found a hand calculator which can calculate into exponents for this example. Don't do this with a simple calculator since you can't add numbers large enough. I randomly picked a number—384,725,872—to add to a second, but larger number, also randomly picked—12,572,485,252. With these two numbers I created the Eng Summation Series! Below are the ratios I obtained:

Eng Summation Series Numbers*	Ratios Between Adjoining Numbers
384,725,872	
12,572,485,252	0.03060062226
12,957,211,120	0.9703079744
25,529,696,370	0.5075348697
38,486,907,490	0.6633345736
64,016,603,860	0.60120119565
102,503,511,400	0.6245308379
166,520,115,300	0.6155623374
269,023,626,700	0.6189796600
435,543,742,000	0.6176730389
704,567,368,700	0.6181718901

*If you work out the numbers, they are actually rounded off; but it's still with 9-digit accuracy! You are welcome to try with your own numbers!

After a while you will see that the ratio between two adjoining numbers approaches 0.618! You can also start off with the first number being larger than the second one, instead of the conventional way, which is to start off with two numbers, the second being larger than the first! The first two numbers will add to a third number which will be larger than either of the first two numbers. From the third number onward, the consecutive numbers will always be larger and you will obtain the orderly increment of the summation series. At the beginning the ratio relationship is erratic, but as the numbers are added together the summation series' ratios approach 0.618.

Regardless of what two numbers you use, they will eventually arrive at a ratio relationship of 0.618!

If you have a spreadsheet program for your computer, try this set of exercises. You'll be amazed that any summation series you can create, without regard to starting points, with this approach, will always, *always* get you to a 0.618 relationship! Meanwhile, Leonardo de Pisa and Eduoard Lucas, get thee behind me!

What About a Negative Number?

Then, I played around with negative numbers! What did I find? If both starting numbers are negative, we immediately obtain a negative number series and the ratio then arrives at a negative 0.618 relationship.

What happens when one of the numbers is negative and the other is positive? Well, let's take a look at what types of negative numbers I'm experimenting with. Let's take the first two numbers of our expected sequence to be 5 and −13! What do we have as ratios?

5, −13, −8, −21, −29: + − − −

−13, 5, −8, −3, −11: − + − −

So after the numbers are added, we get a string of negative numbers.

Let's take a look at a larger negative number whose absolute value is larger than the second number. This is the series we have and even here, eventually the summation series becomes totally positive.

−21, 15, −6, 9, 3: − + − + +

−17, 15, −2, 13, 11, 24, 35: − + − + + +

If we used the first negative number whose absolute value is greater than the second number, this is what we have:

−10, 16, 6, 22: − + + +

The summation series immediately becomes positive.

The unique example above is to take a larger negative number whose absolute value is larger than the second number. Why? Because the initial negative-to-positive oscillation stretches the longest before the sum-

mation series becomes totally positive. What significance is there for this observation? The uniqueness of
the series when it becomes totally positive is more
defined to have been extracted from the first two sets of
numbers. The ratio of 0.618 that we will obtain from the
positive number series derived from these first two numbers is unique. No longer are the positive numbers
related merely by 0.618. They are also related by a
unique starting set of two numbers! The forecasting
ability of this unique set of oscillations is unique!

After evaluating each of the three sets of two numbers, I can conclude the following: eventually, the ratio
between two consecutive numbers will be 0.618 (or a
negative 0.618), regardless of what numbers are used to
start the summation. Making one of the two numbers a
negative number will determine whether or not the ratio
is a positive or a negative number.

The relationship of the two numbers to each other is
important when you are using a negative number.
Depending on how small the negative number is relative
to the second, positive number, you can obtain a summation series which has a series at the beginning of the
series which oscillates between positive and negative
numbers! It is only when you find sets of two numbers
which vary by some value that you will obtain this oscillation between positive and negative; and even here you
will eventually obtain either a completely negative or a
completely positive series! The implications of this
"oscillation facet" of this particular summation series
approach are great!

Implications for Trading

What does this mean for your trading? First, for
those who are not familiar with the application of the
ratio derived from the Fibonacci Summation Series—er,
The Eng Summation Series—other practitioners of the

135

arcane art of numerology have attested that the ratio is found everywhere in nature, including sunflower seeds and seashell spirals! For example, this ratio is also found in market actions and reactions.

Here are my conclusions on the ratio's relevance to your trading:

Conclusion #1. With the Fibonacci Summation Series you were fixed on the numbers in the sequence, i.e., 1, 3, 5, 8, 13. When time or price reversals came at those numbers, the Fibonacci Summation Series accurately forecasted those numbers. But when reversals in time or price came at different numbers, perhaps 1, 3, 4, 7, 11, etc., the Lucas Summation Series could account for them. Then there are the other summation series—Tribonacci or Tetranicci, etc., Summation Series (for more details see *Technical Analysis of Stocks, Options & Futures,* Probus Publishing)— which accounted for other reversals in time and price. Now, with the Eng Summation Series, ALL numbers are significant for reversals, since all the summation series (Fibonacci, Lucas, etc.) are now subsets of this expanded Eng Series!

What can a trader do? A little information is fine, but too much is paralyzing! I've shown you that all numbers can be time or price reversal points because you can arrive at any two consecutive numbers' interrelatedness to each other by the 0.618 ratio. Expand the horizon of your thinking a bit. Even though I've shown (not mathematically, but inductively) that any two numbers in the universe are related to each other by the ratio 0.618, you can use that information to obtain useful forecasts. Start off by simply saying any one number *randomly* picked is related to another *specific* number by the ratio 0.618! Or, the unique summation series can be derived at by varying the sign of one of the two numbers. The resultant summation series is unique.

This is a very powerful conclusion: any number picked from the infinite universe is related to only one specific number by the ratio of 0.618!

At the same time this conclusion is universal in scope, it is also specific in forecast! Universal because you can take any number. Specific because once you perform a function on any universally picked number, the product is specific to that number!

The implications for forecasting are ominous because they are limited. No longer need the trader be tied into specific sets of numbers which the Fibonacci Summation Series implied. **Any number will do ...** but only specific forecasts from any number will be valid!

Conclusion #2. The Chaotic scientist, who believes that everything is related to each other, is that much closer to proving that any action in the universe is related to other actions, much farther removed and physically distant than apparent. Because now any number that is picked, which has significance to someone or something, when acted upon by the ratio 0.618, creates another number which is directly tied into that first number!

Just because we are limited in our scope of observation we have easily dismissed with some of the Chaotic scientists' claims—that all actions in the universe are related to each other—and we were never able to see the action we created in our own local world could affect the rainforests in Brazil!

The trade you made today in soybeans probably is affecting someone out there in the fields of Georgia. He doesn't know it and you can't see it. The spread you placed in Treasury bond futures probably is affecting another person out there in some finance ministry in South America. He doesn't know it, but you're hoping that it is affecting him.

Conclusion #3. Traders who are always looking for more reasons to initiate or not to initiate a trade now really have the mother of all reasons to be more careful: the universe looking down upon them. Be careful; what you do does affect something, somewhere.

More research needs to be done on the uses of the Eng Summation Series. Of course, now that I've written about this series, I'm sure that my action has caused a 0.618 factor result out there. Can you send me notice whether your results are directly related to my action by a factor of 0.618? All right then, how about 0.382? or maybe 0.314? Or . . . .

RULE 23

The Alternation Between Hope and Despondency Is an Underlying Cause of Market Cycles: Movements Both Up and Down Are Overdone

Everything eventually gets overdone or underdone. In the markets, you can get the public into a buying frenzy or into a selling panic relatively easily. This chapter will show you how I learned this fact years ago.

I cut my teeth on commodities trading in 1973 when I became a member of the Chicago Open Board of Trade, now known as the MidAmerica Commodity Exchange (MidAm).

After I learned the game of floor scalping, I progressed to the Chicago Board of Trade in the late 1970s. Shortly thereafter, I sold my seat at the MidAmerica Commodity Exchange.

After I traded bond futures at the Board for several years, the commodities community started the idea of trading options against futures. This came on the heels of the successful creation of the largest stock options exchange in the world, Chicago Board Options Exchange, back in 1973. The futures traders wanted to duplicate the same success.

The MidAmerica Opportunity for Futures Options Trading

I reasoned that options on futures would take off just as it took off in the stock market. Where could I position myself to take advantage of this fact? I already had a membership on a stock options market and one at the Board. I concluded that the MidAmerica Commodity Exchange could stand to benefit from the implementation of options on futures! I put in a bid for a seat, and on April 20, 1982, I became an owner of a seat at MidAm.

So as a proud owner of a MidAm seat, I did exactly what most people do when they invest—I bought first and analyzed later. In psychological terms, I satiated my emotional need and then looked for the rationalizations. I started to analyze, in much greater depth, the impact of futures options on the exchanges, on the volume, on strategies, etc. The research results were always positive and always bullish.

One Fact I Overlooked While Researching

Except for one minor detail that I obtained by accident. I asked a MidAm official who later went over to the Chicago Board of Trade as an economist what he thought of my investment. He corroborated every one of my points with one exception concerning leverage: There was no benefit to owning futures options versus the futures contracts themselves when it came to gaining leverage. In fact "margin" on futures contracts was less than the cost of the options themselves. In the stock market, owning stock entailed a maximum margin of 50 percent versus owning options on the stocks, which often brought the margin down to less than 10 percent. However, unlike the stock market, options on futures would not have that leverage because the margin on futures ran consistently between 3–10 percent to begin with. For these reasons, this economist argued that futures options would not trade as actively as stock options. No matter how many facts and figures one extracts, why do we overlook that one detail that will cause our . . . my downfall?

Membership Price Drops as Exchange Gears Up for Options

Well, I was long a seat and couldn't do anything about it. The futures options was going to trade on a certain date but was delayed twice. The price of my seat at the MidAm went down and down. I had bought it at $14,750 and by this time it was trading at $8,500, a mark-to-market loss of over $6,000. Although it didn't matter too much because I was making money at the Board, the loss still bothered me. So, I patiently waited for the futures options to start trading. I wasn't worried because I knew I was on a lucky cycle high. I felt something would happen to salvage my investment.

I waited for the onset of futures options to start trading so that my analyses could be vindicated. While waiting, I delved into exchange politics and fundamentals. The MidAm is a nice little exchange, but nothing has ever happened to it. Membership prices never went above $27,000. With this little seat you could trade practically all the markets. No public business ever went to the MidAm; the floor brokers could not make a living from brokerage executions so the price of the seat stayed low. A general rule of thumb is that a membership on an exchange, regardless of what type, trades at about 125 percent of the yearly income of an executing floor broker. This means that if a seat is trading at about $100,000, then you can be reasonably certain that the average floor broker is making about $80,000 a year in income. This is the only rule of thumb that I've been able to discover. Note that this does not consider what a floor *trader* makes since the floor trader's income depends less on order flow and more on the trader's own acumen and capital resources.

Based on this, the MidAm floor brokers were making about 80 percent of the market valuation of between $14,750 and $8,000, or between $11,800 and $6,400 a year in floor brokerage income.

So, it came as no surprise to me that the members were annoyed that no public orders came into the exchange to keep all the floor traders alive. Well, I sat back and saw that about 1,200 members of the MidAm were fighting to make a buck on the exchange's order flow, which was considerably less than at the larger exchanges, so the MidAm needed to do something to change the equation. The exchange had pushed as hard as it could to increase order flow but was unsuccessful.

About a year later on June 30, 1983, the exchange hiked up dues, clearing fees, and badge fees. Ouch! An exchange with no volume because of no public business will now hike up fees? Their apparent philosophy was to squeeze the captive membership audience a little more!

MidAmerica Buys the Chicago Mercantile Exchange Building

The expenses were mounting. In a July 7, 1983, letter to members, the exchange announced they were purchasing the Chicago Mercantile Exchange building and its trading floor at 444 W. Jackson (see Figure 23.1). With all the rosy forecasts and additional revenue projections the exchange sold its membership on the move.

I deemed it to be bullish, if played right. In the worse case scenario I considered it bearish to neutral if nothing happened to the MidAm once the exchange moved into the new building. The Chicago Mercantile Exchange building was built on leased land with a 99-year lease. Even if the exchange wasn't able to take advantage of the increased physical capacity to conduct more business, the leasehold value of the land was worth more than the purchase price of the building plus the land. How could the MidAm lose?

My Plan for Members To Make More Money

Now that the exchange was going to have increased revenues because of all the bullish factors, I still wondered how the members were going to make a living. Was there going to be increased order flow whereby the pit broker could execute orders and make a decent living? Was there going to be successful marketing campaigns to get the exchange more public orders? These were a few of the many questions that popped up in my mind.

Then, as a twist to the issue of creating more income for members, I thought the unthinkable other side of the equation: What about cutting down the number of members? I reasoned that there should be fewer members fighting for the fixed number of orders coming into the pit.

But how could fewer memberships be accomplished? The value of the seats were higher than when they were sold by the exchange many years ago in a treasury offering to raise working capital. Since the exchange had no cash, it could not buy back the memberships.

I reasoned the exchange could implement a reverse-seat split! I devised a plan whereby the exchange could effectively lower the number of memberships from the market and not have to spend a dime to do it. Since I devised the plan, the Chicago Board of Trade and the MidAm, several years later, have implemented them without publicly acknowledging me about this.

143

So I'm long this seat at $14,750. It's trading between $8,000 and $9,000. The MidAm has problems with too many memberships. The futures options are scheduled to trade soon at the MidAm. How was I to execute all that is known to my benefit? Try to sell the exchange on the idea of doing the reverse-stock split, of course!

Gathering Support for My Idea

Since the members were getting irate over the lack of upward movement in their seat investments a group of disenchanted members started a campaign to remove the current officials from office. They created the MidAmerica Floor Traders' Association specifically to promote their candidates. The issues with which they were most disenchanted with were encapsulated in the letter to all members: Exchange expenses needed to be cut, membership dues had to be reduced, the exchange needed to involve more members, membership and management needed to communicate more, and the exchange needed to have more public and industry profiles.

The question now was to determine which avenue was the most expedient in getting what I wanted to accomplish: causing a reverse-seat split. Do I approach the current officials who have vested interests in maintaining the status quo, or do I approach the disenchanted members who would like changes? Of course, I would go to the disenchanted members and consult them on the idea. But first, in deference to the current officials I contacted the exchange chairman at the time, Brian Connelly. I called Brian several times at home to discuss this and he said he needed something written from me before he could present it to the exchange board. He thought it was a great idea!

I had drafted a letter detailing the reverse-seat split. (See Figure 23.2.)

144

Human Nature Haunts Me Again

While I was waiting word from the current officials, I addressed these four letters to the board members and sealed them in three envelopes. One envelope I "accidentally" left unsealed. Instead of leaving it for the exchange secretary to present to these board members I gave them to one of the disenchanted members seeking office in the forthcoming election. I instructed him to find these four board members and hand them the proposals. I only hinted that it contained a very beneficial proposal to exchange members and that it must be kept secret. I told one member that I was discussing something of importance to the membership with the board members and I would reveal this information to the general membership later.

I had set up the environment for something to happen, but I didn't know exactly what. The board rejected the idea, so I returned to the Chicago Board of Trade to continue trading bond futures, patiently waiting for the day futures options would trade at the MidAm. Actually, I kept myself so busy that I didn't have time to fret about the bad investment at the MidAm.

A Bullish Run on Memberships!

Several weeks later I checked out what was going on at the MidAm. By this time, the seat price had popped up to $17,500! This was a phenomenal gain of about $8,000 to $9,000 in a matter of a few weeks. I wondered what had happened.

I had a profit on my seat of about $3,000 if I were to sell at the market. The old high was around $25,000 to $27,000. I looked for the seat to challenge those highs. Once a trend is in motion it tends to stay in motion. I now monitored the bid and ask of the seat prices every day. Instead of challenging the old highs it topped out at

$17,500 and proceeded to go down. Should I sell? Decisions, decisions.

At the Right Time, At the Right Place

One day I was on the phone with the exchange secretary of the MidAm getting a fix on the membership prices. The bid was now $12,700 and offered at $13,000, which was a drop of about $4,000 from the recent high. This was getting very exciting. While chatting with the secretary, she put me on hold so she could talk to a member who bought an additional seat at $17,500 on the runup. When she came back on the line, she told me that she was concerned for this member because he had told her that he couldn't afford to pay for the membership. Voila! This was a signal of some sort.

Here was a classic example of overdoing things: A membership buyer on the high of the move saying he couldn't afford to pay for it. Who would buy a seat and not be able to pay for it? Was I goofy or what? Did I have to have a telegram sung to me that this had been a top? This was a sure sign of an overextension. What was I waiting for? Options on futures? Nah, they'd never go. The Chicago Board of Trade buying out the MidAm? Nah, they'd never want the liability. Within the hour I was in front of the exchange's secretary desk instructing her to hit the bid of $12,700 on the membership. She tried to talk me out of it, strongly suggesting that I place an offer behind the current $13,000 offer. But I learned a long time ago that if I wanted to get out of my losing positions I should go out at the market, with no scrounging around for pennies when the position I'm holding is not good!

For whatever reasons the seat prices popped up (I think I have a rough idea), for whatever reasons I was on the phone listening about a poorly capitalized trader (I had to monitor my investments, don't you think?), and for whatever reasons those events came to be that morning, I said to her: "Hit the bid and talk to me later."

It was my money, my decision, my execution. (See Figure 23.3.)

The seat then proceeded to trade down past $8,000, down past $7,000 and it even touched $3,500 recently. By this time I had received my check and smarting from the $2,250 loss. Darn, I wish I had been able to sell it at $15,000, but at least I didn't wait and lose even more.

There was no reason for the memberships to pop up to $17,500 nor was there a reason for them to trade down to $3,500. The two extremes were way out of line! This example illustrates perfectly that at times you might know the reasons for either, but most likely you won't ever know why. How many people really did know why those seats popped up? In this particular case, I think I have a very good idea of what caused the over-bought conditions. In any case, keep in mind that markets get overdone and underdone.

Epilogue: The futures options finally did trade, and the MidAm sold itself to the Chicago Board of Trade for a pittance. On the events surrounding the reverse-split idea, the Chicago Board of Trade implemented this concept in their Associates Memberships several years later. The MidAm eventually did do a reverse-split on their seats close to ten years later.

FIGURE 23.1 Front of letter dated July 7, 1983

MidAmerica Commodity Exchange

The Marketplace for MiniContracts
175 West Jackson Boulevard
Chicago, Illinois 60604
(312) 435-0606

July 7, 1983

Dear Member:

Late in 1982, the Board of Directors was faced with an important decision:
either spend $1.3 million to upgrade the current trading facility, knowing
that even after this expenditure the number of new contracts, clearing firms
and floor traders would soon be limited because of trading space; or, invest
$2 million to buy a $20 million facility which would provide for unlimited
growth. As you know, based upon the facts and figures, the Board determined
that purchasing the New MidAmerica Building was the only responsible course of
action. With this decision, an irreversible commitment to the future was
made. Although the past nine years have recorded the Exchange's growth into
and out of its present facility, future growth must continue at an even
faster, more accelerated pace.

Vital to the fulfillment of the commitment to growth is increased marketing.
As a result of our current and planned programs, we expect volume to increase
substantially over the next few years. First, within a few months of the move
we anticipate doubling the number of products now offered. Second, quotation
subscriptions are rising steadily. Now over 3,500 locations carry MidAmerica
quotes throughout the world. Our quotes not only provide revenue but, more
importantly, serve as a self-supporting marketing tool, when coupled with
publication in the <u>Wall Street Journal</u>. More visibility means more business!

Finally, our new marketing program will promote aggressively new and existing
contracts to account executives, commodity trading advisors, and commodity
pool operators through direct mail, personal calls and seminars, as well as
through <u>Wall Street Journal</u> and Commodities magazine advertisements. There is
no lack of opportunity within the futures industry! -- and our marketing
objectives recognize this!

Expanded facilities and increased marketing commitments comprise the only
direction your Board could have taken, and additional resources, both human
and financial will be required. With this knowledge and a firm understanding
of its bold objectives, the Board approved an operating budget for the coming
fiscal year of $4.3 million, and accordingly increased member dues, clearing
fees and other charges as explained in the enclosed notice.

148

FIGURE 23.1 (continued) Back of letter dated July 7, 1983

The $1.1 million increase over last year's budget includes:

- increased occupancy expense, as anticipated, of $508,000;
- additional services to the floor, including price information systems of $44,000;
- an additional $185,000 for the trading of new contracts, maintenance of electronic boards, and the development and implementation of an in-house clearing system;
- an increase of $135,000 to the marketing budget as proposed by the New Products and Business Development Committee;
- one-time expenses of $80,000 for moving, equipment installation, etc;
- the balance of $145,000 to cover all other expenses including those subject to an inflation factor (estimated at 5 percent).

In arriving at the projected occupancy expense, 65 percent of the Chicago Mercantile Exchange's 1982 building operating expenses were allocated to MidAmerica's FY'84 budget. This reduction takes into consideration our anticipated floor population and proportionately reduced utilities. Very favorable proposals for maintenance contracts and housekeeping of the building have been obtained. Despite these economies there are two fixed costs, real estate taxes and the air rights lease, which must be incurred full-force.

While anticipated building operating expenses will constitute substantial increases over this past year, they represent very little difference from what the Exchange would have had to spend had it remained at 175 W. Jackson. The Tilton & Lewis (architects/engineers) study of the feasibility of renovating our present floor to meet immediate and future needs had to assume leasing the entire second floor and rebuilding the trading floor. Further, estimates were that this expansion would be adequate only until 1990 at best. Coupling leasehold improvements with greatly increased rents resulting from the renegotiation of expiring leases at much higher rates would have made annual occupancy costs estimated at $780,000 only moderately less than the $925,000 projected for the new building.

When dues and fees were last increased in 1980, the goal was to maintain a balanced budget and grow at a steady pace. This we did. Now, three years later, we are faced with greater demands. Our immediate plan is focused on the aggressive pursuit of increased business to ensure full use of the New MidAmerica Building. Presenting a premier facility has built-in advantages already at work for us. It increases our visibility, enhances our image, and strengthens our position in the marketplace. All of these things will add up to more opportunities for you, the member. The Exchange has arrived in the mid-1980s with a strong financial base and a multi-million dollar building. This base must be kept strong while the benefits of the building become fully maximized.

With your continued support, MidAmerica will realize its full potential bringing success and rewards to all of its members.

Sincerely,

Brian J. Connelly
Chairman

David H. Morgan
President

FIGURE 23.2 Page 1 of 4 of proposal

MIDAMERICA COMMODITY EXCHANGE
MEMBERSHIP REORGANIZATION PROPOSAL

I, a member of the MidAmerica Commodity Exchange, would like to offer a proposal for the reorganization of the memberships of the exchange. After several meetings and telephone conversations with Mr. Brian J. Connelly, Chairman of MidAmerica Commodity Exchange, I have arrived at a concrete proposal to present to the membership.

My proposal is a very simple one. I would like to suggest to the membership that we, as members, reorganize our exchange membership so that we may have less outstanding memberships through the following program: I propose that we have a <u>reverse</u> <u>split</u> of our memberships. The following details what has to be done and how it can be done.

First, some pertinent data concerning the present state of memberships. There are 1205 memberships outstanding; these memberships were sold by the exchange at prices below $7000. The number of memberships is more than enough to satisfy current market demand for trading privileges on our exchange. The market price of a MidAmerica Commodity Exchange membership is $9800 (as of July 22, 1983).

I propose to the membership that anyone who wishes to purchase a membership on the MidAmerica Commodity Exchange in order to trade or represent others as floor brokers on the exchange be required to purchase $1\frac{1}{2}$ memberships. In other words, a prospective new member may not purchase one membership by paying the current price and then having the membership transferred to him by the selling member, but that the prospective new member must purchase $1\frac{1}{2}$ memberships in order to be a member of the exchange. As the number of prospective new members purchase memberships from current members, the actual number of full memberships outstanding with trading privileges will decrease from the current 1205 to 803.33 (the fractional membership will be dealt with by the exchange in an appropriate manner).

To faciliate the transfer of "memberships," a DEADLINE DATE for the implementation of this new requirement for prospective new members will be determined at a time in the near future.

FIGURE 23.2 (continued) Page 2 of 4 of proposal

Prior to the DEADLINE DATE memberships will continue to be sold and bought in the present manner. After the DEADLINE DATE, all members who own memberships will have a MidAmerica Commodity Exchange membership to transact business with. If these members wish to sell their memberships after the DEADLINE DATE, they must register such memberships for sale with the exchange. In return, the prospective selling member will be given 2 UNITS OF MEMBERSHIP, for each full membership, to sell or hold. This "member" may sell both UNITS OF MEMBERSHIP at the same time, or the selling member may retain one for speculative purposes. Once the member registers his full membership for sale and is given 2 UNITS OF MEMBERSHIP by the exchange to sell, he no longer has any trading privileges on the exchange.

After the DEADLINE DATE the exchange will no longer hold a bid/ask market in full memberships; instead, the exchange will hold a bid/ask market in UNITS OF MEMBERSHIP.

After the DEADLINE DATE any prospective new member who desires to acquire membership trading privileges on the exchange must place bids in the UNITS OF MEMBERSHIP market that the exchange will maintain. The prospective new member must now purchase 3 UNITS OF MEMBERSHIP and register such acquisitions with the exchange in order to become a member.

Mr. Brian J. Connelly suggests that anyone who owns any UNITS OF MEMBERSHIP be liable for dues in a proportionate amount. I would like to point out that the following is more conducive to tightening of such UNITS OF MEMBERSHIP supply: anyone who owns 1 UNITS OF MEMBERSHIP, and not more than 1, should be given a release from payment of the respective portion of dues. Anyone who owns more than 1 UNITS OF MEMBERSHIP must pay respective dues on each UNITS OF MEMBERSHIP owned above one. This will remove the negative cost of carry on the one UNITS OF MEMBERSHIP owned per individual. The person owning only 1 UNITS OF MEMBERSHIP can keep it off the market easier, again decreasing the supply of UNITS OF MEMBERSHIPS for sale, and resultantly, make it more difficult for prospective new members from completing full memberships.

FIGURE 23.2 (continued) Page 3 of 4 of proposal

A member who owns a membership on the exchange prior to the DEADLINE DATE and then sells one of his 2 UNITS OF MEMBERSHIP after the DEADLINE DATE, would still retain 1 UNITS OF MEMBERSHIP. This one UNITS OF MEMBERSHIP will not allow the owner to trade on the exchange. If the 1 UNITS OF MEMBERSHIP owner then decides to become a member of the exchange again, he will now have to purchase 2 more UNITS OF MEMBERSHIP to become a member of the exchange. This person, despite the fact that he was a full member prior to the DEADLINE DATE will still have to purchase 2 additional UNITS OF MEMBERSHIP because he had split his full membership into UNITS OF MEMBERSHIP for sale.

The following are the ramifications of this proposal. By splitting the full memberships into UNITS OF MEMBERSHIP for sale, more members will be removed from the trading floor population. The projected increase in contracts volume in the new commodities to be traded (e.g., foreign currencies, other precious metals, etc.) and the new commodities options on our expanded list of underlying commodities (e.g., gold, etc.) will be spread among fewer members on the floor of the exchange who have retained their trading privileges by not splitting their memberships. More money will be made by the members who are on the floor who have left their memberships intact. The value, intrinsic and monetary, of our memberships will increase. With our members financially healthy, the exchange will grow rapidly.

The proposal outlined above is simple and to the point. It is designed to reduce the number of memberships outstanding at the MidAmerica Commodity Exchange. The reduction will come at the expense of the prospective new members, which it rightfully must be. The old and current members have borne the cost of exchange expansion and to have new prospective members become full members with full trading privileges without exacting a cost from them would be grossly unfair to the old and current members. At the same time, coinciding the DEADLINE DATE with the move to the new MidAmerica Commodity Exchange building will support memberships further. Timing the move with the acquisition of more commodities and options to trade at the

---

FIGURE 23.2 (continued) Page 4 of 4 of proposal

MidAmerica Commodity Exchange will be even more bullish for the memberships. With the increased prices for membership privileges, public recognition will increase also.

In closing this proposal, I would like to credit Mr. Brian J. Connelly with hearing me out and offering his own ideas for this proposal for the reorganization of the exchange. If the membership is amenable to this proposal, I would like to have the opportunity to serve on the committee which will be designated for the implementation of this proposal.

Sincerely,

William F. Ng

July 25, 1983

FIGURE 23.3 Letter detailing my sale at $12,700

MidAmerica Commodity Exchange

The Marketplace for MiniContracts
175 West Jackson Boulevard
Chicago, Illinois 60604
(312) 435-0606

December 7, 1983

Mr. William F. Ng

Dear Mr. Ng:

Per our letter to you of November 28, 1983, the enclosed check in the
amount of twelve thousand fifty-eight and .33/100 dollars represents
the net proceeds from the sale of your membership calculated as follows:

Gross sales price:	$12,700.00
Less processing fee:	- 500.00
Dues owed:	- 141.67
NET PROCEEDS:	$12,058.33

If you have not already completed and returned the questionnaire
recently sent to you, another copy is enclosed. We would appreciate
its return as soon as possible.

Please let us know if we can be of further assistance to you.

Sincerely,
MIDAMERICA COMMODITY EXCHANGE

Nancy R. Godfrey
Assistant Vice President/Member Services

NRG/DsG

Encl.

RULE 24

Judge Corporate Officials on Company Performance, Not on How They Treat Employees or the Public

Most of what company insiders do when it comes to their company will never be seen or known by investors like you or me. As long as these officials follow a simple course of generating profits to allow the company to expand you shouldn't even care what they do.

Most of what corporate officials say to the public falls in the category of pandering to the public. That's why companies have stockholder relations departments. They don't exist to make profits for you; they exist to keep you misinformed on what the companies are really doing.

However, if this corporate official is any good as a manager of the company that you invest in, you might want to use him to your advantage by allowing him or her to do the job you won't do or can't do. In this sense, these corporate officials are working for you. Your investment in these companies is an implied endorsement of their activities. Regardless how some of these corporate heads might treat their employees, your primary concern is how well the company performs.

Let's take several cases to point out how you, as an investor, can use the distance you have from the company to your benefit.

For example, a well-known electronics retailing firm has made money for me year in and year out. As a stockholder I like the company. No matter how they treat employees or how poor and expensive their products are, or how terrible their service is, they have increased their sales every year for the last ten years I've owned their stock. They are phenomenal marketers, and they basically cater to buyers with their local stores in small towns throughout the country. This is a captive audience. This company was one of the very first to get a foothold in the personal computer market, but they lost that lead because they considered themselves to be marketers of products. They are merchandisers.

I've benefited handsomely with this company. I go into their stores and chat with the employees and commiserate with them on how badly they get paid, how terrible their electronic equipment is, how their current computers can't match price and performance with other personal computer clones, and I always walk away feeling that the company management will probably burn in hell one of these days. Yet, I get my dividend checks which have constantly been growing. The stock has tripled since I invested in it. I'm happy.

This is the same with the SIN stocks—alcohol distillers and cigarette manufacturers. I have no qualms about investing in these companies. Even if the corporate heads are paid high salaries to run companies which deal specifically in products and services which are known to be detrimental to the users' health, I would be foolish not to take a profitable position within these companies because I have an ethical consideration. As long as I don't smoke or drink, that's fine with me. You might ask whether or not I'm deliberately abetting the immorality and harming the users of their products or services by investing in these companies. As a matter of fact, I traded soybeans for years without ever seeing one or ever knowing that soybeans were used in the development of toxic chemicals.

What about defense companies? Or, companies that make war machinery?

As an investor and trader I've bought and sold stocks in Lockheed, Litton Industries, and other war machinery related companies. I've never gone to the trouble of discussing management policies with corporate officials. I leave it up to them. Somebody's got to do it. Better that they run and manage the companies than me.

Since I have a live and let live attitude toward how officials run their company, I judge them only on their performance. They have their agendas and I have mine. Their agenda is to run a company which can be as unpopular as current society deems. My agenda is to be careful with my money and pick the stock that will grow.

RULE 25

The Long-Term Trend of the Market Is Always Bullish Because the Losers Fade Away

Markets are bullish, but not bullish enough for you and me to make much money in. What I've discovered about blatantly obvious statements such as these is that upon further investigation they really aren't that obvious. Just because the long-term averages go up doesn't mean that the average person will make any profits. The reason is more subtle than the average investor's ability to select profitable investments.

Several years ago I met one of the slickest salesmen in the commodity business I have had the bad fortune to ever know. This salesman had found a very slick way to give the impression that his buy and sell recommendations were always profitable. By accident he backed his way into an extremely profitable trading system. What happened to this salesman illustrates how his own impatience caused him to destroy his system.

In his promotional campaigns on the national finance station, FNN/CNBC cable television, he had created commercials offering his free newsletter. In this newsletter he made and then tracked his recommendations to buy and sell certain commodities.

He showed me his newsletter and was very proud of it. He pointed out the table that tracked the recommendations. I looked at the open trade profits and losses and was surprised that the profits were huge and the losses were small. I blurted out to him that he must have been doing something right to get these results.

He quietly told me the newsletter was one of his best marketing tools he had for selling his brokerage services. He designed the newsletter to be a promotional piece which showed huge profits and small losses.

As he was telling me this, I wondered to myself that it took me many years of hard-earned experience in the markets finally to be able to get to the point of being able to hang onto winners and cut my losers. Here was someone selling a trading methodology which racked up huge profits and small losses. He implied to me that he had absolute control of his market positions. He told me he cranked out these results every day with great ease!

As I engaged in further discussion with him, he revealed his little "secret" to me.

In a weak moment of revelation, he said, "Bill, there's nothing hard to learn about the system. Even though the system shows so well, I'm still losing money year after year."

Now I was even more puzzled. He continued, "What I do is this, Bill. After I've randomly picked out a market to get into, I put on the trade. The trade can then show a profit or it can show a loss. I guarantee you that in about three days, I will either have a $300 winner in that trade or a $300 loser. None of my losing trades stay on my books for more than three days. The winning trade I leave alone. As long as the open position shows a profit I don't close it out. Because I don't close it out, it shows up as open trade equity in my recommended commodities list. The closed trades no longer continue to show on the list and the losses from them are clumped together into one losing number. Meanwhile, I have these huge open trade profits. This looks real good to the prospective client."

I mused to myself that this salesman was doing exactly what a good trader should do: let his profits run and cut his losses. The irony was that the salesman didn't know what he had done. He had accidentally gotten himself into the only profitable trading and investing strategy that I know. For the wrong reason—that he wanted to show huge profits and no open trade losses by removing the losers based on a three-day holding period—he was past the hardest part of trading (cutting losses and running with winners).

Being the devil's advocate I asked him about the comparison of his current equity to starting capital. Surely the newsletter recipients would see that the capital was being drawn down due to market losses. He said the recipients seldom paid attention to those numbers. They were enthralled most of the time with the huge open profits! And, he told me, to track the drawdowns, the recipients must have more than two issues of the newsletter. Most only had one issue before they became this broker's clients. If they got two or more, the broker would have endeared himself to them already; by then, the prospective client was on a first-name basis with the broker.

He was losing money overall because his trade selections were pretty bad: He randomly picked trades. His percentage of winners to losers trade-by-trade probably was considerably less than 50 percent.

Meanwhile, his public record of open positions showed phenomenal profits, which razzled and dazzled the prospective clients.

The markets are essentially what this salesman had lucked into.

160

How can the market be generally bullish when most of us who've ever invested in stocks have owned stocks which went lower after we bought them? What about all those turkeys? In fact, a lot of those stocks have gone sour. So how can anyone agree that the markets are generally bullish?

Let's look at how this is so. The stock market is presently composed of about 8000 stocks in the United States. Not all of these stocks were trading ten years ago. And 20 years ago, not all those stocks were trading then either. This can be dragged further back to when the New York Stock Exchange was founded. Over the course of the market's history more stocks have disappeared or have not gone anywhere than have remained on the exchange; however, the current formulas to account for them do not incorporate these "failed" companies.

You get my point: every day more new stocks are traded. Tomorrow another handful of new stocks will be traded. Meanwhile, the stocks which have gone down and all which have gone bankrupt will be replaced by ones that go up, until even then the time comes for these latter arrival bullish stocks to go down themselves.

What happens to the stocks which go bad? What about the bankruptcies? Well, these stocks fall gracefully and eventually go to zero. Then they're removed from our consciousness.

Have you ever tried to find out what happened to one of your penny stocks which was last trading at 1 cent a share after a 50-cent selloff? I wish you luck! You will have better luck finding a stock certificate from these companies from collectors and dealers in stock certificates than from the transfer agents.

The bad stocks are like the commodities trades which show losses in three days for our salesman. They are removed. Stricken from our thoughts and never to be mentioned again. This is as close as you will ever get to Darwinism of stocks.

The stocks that go from a small office machine company to IBM or from Haloid Corporation to Xerox Corporation, are the stocks that stick with us as time goes by. We hear and read about these stocks all the time. These upwardly mobile stocks stay in our consciousness for years because they are around for years.

Similarly to our salesman's newsletter continued display of his commodity trades with his huge open trade profits, the stocks that are winners are on the books and are displayed to the public. They're listed in the financial pages everyday. Analysts are always writing reports about them. Stockbrokers are always promoting them. You can hardly find anybody working in the business who doesn't have a story about them.

No wonder the vast majority of stock players have shown losses while the rest of the world was truthfully observing the Dow Jones Industrials and the S&P 500 making new historical highs. The past ten years have been the most bullish in our 200-year history. In the context of our own generation, anybody who bought stock 10 years ago has made huge profits. In the rest of the past 200 years, which are more "normal," the majority of stock owners have lost money on stock selection.

So the newsletter is just like the stock market—bullish in appearances only. Bullish in appearance only because the losers never hang around long enough after their demise to be factored into the equations. The winning stocks and commodities will continually be in the public eye.

The solution to mitigating your trading losses is to pick better markets to buy or sell. The solution is not to accept typical statements, such as markets have always gone up and you can't go wrong if you invest from a broad base from the long side in a historically "obviously" bullish trending market. Nothing is further from the truth.

Unlike the salesman who didn't know what he had stumbled onto, you are now aware that all you need to do is to pick better stocks for the right reasons. This means that you, as the owner of the portfolio of stocks, must toss out bad stocks in your portfolio, just as our salesman had done so with his bad recommendations. I wonder, as an aside, what the academics who have performed portfolio studies over the course of many years would obtain as total overall results if they had factored in all stocks traded, not just the ones that remain. The ones that get tossed out will have a dampening effect on overall bullishness of the markets. (Perhaps the investment return on stocks should then be equivalent to those of commodities since the bad stocks would not be eliminated, just as commodities price performance is always included in commodities returns.)

This also means you can't continue to believe that since the markets have gone up a majority of investors have been making money.

RULE 26

Newer Mechanical Timing or Trading Formulas No Longer Preclude Selling at the Top or Buying at the Bottom

When the rule, "mechanical timing or trading formulas preclude selling at the top or buying at the bottom," was discovered in the early 1900s the use of timing techniques was not as advanced as it is now. This rule is no longer true.

In the past, when this observation was made, no extensive work had been done on timing cycles because all information used was based on historical perspectives: open, high, low, close, and day of trading data.

This data was available only after the markets created these numbers, i.e., after the trading day had ended. As a result of the limited amount and type of data available, most previously developed technical analysis techniques simply *followed* trends.

To be able to sell the top or buy the bottom of any market you need a mechanical timing or trading formula that would forecast trend-reversals.

There have been ineffective attempts at taking the same data for trend-following analyses and applying it to methods and formulas which purported to show trend-reversals. This category of indicators is strictly momentum studies (relative strength, stochastics, etc.). These studies attempt to forecast price reversals based on decreasing rate of changes in the underlying prices of stocks or futures you're tracking. The logic is that if the rate of change of one set of price analysis versus another set of price analysis is decreasing then you can infer that the market price is about to reverse.

Most of the time the manipulation of such historical data to create momentum reversals will generate trade decisions which cannot stand the test of market action: one sells into a bull market, or one buys into a bear market.

The only way that I can see where you can attempt to sell the market's high or buy the market's low is to be able to forecast in advance some likely market stage reversals in time. Time is the only factor you can forecast in advance. **This I guarantee you.**

You can use only one set of data to determine market highs or lows: price and volume action defined by specific times from a time series or day of transactions.

When you use only trend-following techniques you only need as many datapoints as the maximum calls for in your analytical formulas. For example, if you are looking for breakouts of a 15-day moving average versus a 34-day moving average, you would really need only 35 days of daily data to generate the 34-day moving average. Anything over 35 days of data would be wasted because your formulas could only use 34 days of data.

However, this is not the case when you use time cycles to forecast price reversals. The reversal points can be found at any time in the future depending on the length of your cycles. If you are looking for 13-day trending cycles, you need multiples of 13 days of data. The more repetitions you are able to find of 13-day cycle peaks and troughs, the more valid the 13-day cycle becomes in forecasting future reversals.

Since there are other length cycles, e.g., 21-day cycles, 55-day cycles, etc., you will find yourself needing a greater and greater amount of time series data. To get meaningful time data to research market reversals you have to have many occurrences of price and volume activity.

For example, cyclical studies based on time data for 200 days of market activity are less valid than 400 days of activity; 400 days are less valid than 1000 days, ad infinitum. The obvious problem with dealing with time analyses is the researcher has to have a lot of data.

Now, with the advent of computerized technology you can analyze lots of data to forecast time reversals. In the past, no computers were used and the lack of time to conduct the analyses made cyclical studies inexact.

The methods of forecasting price reversals in time is at the beginning stages of development. Why is this so? The mass of analyses do not have the luxury of large databases and computing power to analyze that data till recently. At this point we are at the leading edge of developing time forecasting formulas and techniques.

I fully expect that within ten years more techniques will be developed using timing cycles to forecast imminent price reversals than in the past fifty years. Just as the automobile's development opened up myriad possibilities of benefits, this application of computers to time series analyses will cause our knowledge base to grow in leaps and bounds.

When the ancient Romans adopted the Arabic numbering system and depended less on their own numeral system, their ability to carry on importing and exporting operations increased many times. Similarly, so will the adoption of timing cycles studies increase our own personal abilities to see future events from the backdrop of past events.

166

Conventional Methodology During the Pre-Computer Era

Generally there are two types of a trending markets: bullish and bearish. The markets are either trending bullishly or bearishly 30 percent of the time. You can trade breakouts of the trend when the market starts, unfolds, and ends.

The other market type is the trading range market. This occurs 70 percent of the time. When this market is unfolding you can trade it by selling the high and buying the lows.

In both types of markets—trending or trading—it is not necessary to pick the timing of the trades to make money. This is because trending markets tend to stay in trending type action so that if you miss the exact moment of breakout you still have ample time to get on board either the next day or shortly thereafter. In trading markets, if you miss the exact moment of reversal and get on board shortly thereafter the amount of loss of potential profit will be relatively small because the range of trading markets are narrow, i.e., you can't get hurt too much.

Another reason is that markets in pre-computer times were not as price volatile as they are, now that computers are used more frequently. Others are using computers to enhance their market analyses even though you might not be.

The timing is not important for different reasons for different types of markets. Trending markets because you can always get on board shortly thereafter. Trading markets because you can never get hurt too badly if you enter at the wrong pricing. However, most aggressive traders have discovered that if they use analytical hardware to obtain more buying and selling points they also increase their profitable trading opportunities. This explains why these traders have found another niche to expand profitable opportunities using more datapoints.

167

Refined Methodology During the Computer Era

The refined methodology for applying technical analyses means you must buy at the bottom of a trading range, immediately prior to an upside breakout of a trading range. It also means you must sell immediately prior to a breakdown out of a trading range.

With the amount of increasing global liquidity in tradeable markets, it is very easy to take on huge positions and not really know their impacts if the market were to lurch either up or down. With a one point loss in a position of 100 shares, the trader loses only $100. With the same one point loss on 100,000 shares, however, this trader will lose $100,000. Because of the "increasing equity risk attributable to increased position risk," traders are seeking methods and ways to even reduce this compound risk by trying to buy at the very low price and sell at the very high price of a market's move. The more successful a trader is in finding these precise points, the less he will need capital since there is less risk of losses. But by emphasizing this component of trading, the trader himself fails to recognize the need for conservative trade management and feels more comfortable putting more money at risk. Unfortunately, this facade veils the skills needed to trade successfully.

In Figure 26.1, in the conventional methodology you bought at points 1, 2, 3, 4, ... X. However, the refined methodology allows the analyst to buy at point X, just prior to the breakout to the upside.

In Figure 26.2, the conventional methodology instructed you to sell at points 1, 2, 3, 4, ... X. Again, the refined method allows the analyst to sell at point X, just prior to the breakout to the downside.

Leading edge traders use advanced chaos analyses which permit the analyst to find points X, at which, in the jargon of chaotic and nonlinear market action models, there is a phase shift which forces the data series into another fractal. Of all the buy points from 1 to X, at that particular point in TIME of point X, the market shifts into a different level of activity.

From my own experience in trying to uncover the "fractal bifurcation point" of market stages, I have discovered phenomenal success at times and dismal failure at other times. Even if I attempt to use the factor of "time" as a decision-making tool in my market analyses, there also is a time to use the element of time for forecasting! There's a time to use time as a decision-making tool.

FIGURE 26.1 Conventional Methodology (You Buy at Points 1, 2, 3, 4, . . . X.) versus Refined Methodology (You Buy at Point X.)

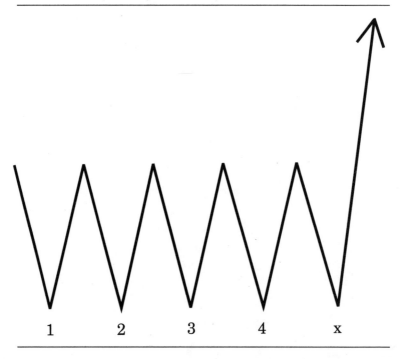

FIGURE 26.2 Conventional Methodology (You Sell at Points 1, 2, 3, 4, . . . X.) versus Refined Methodology (You Buy at Point X.)

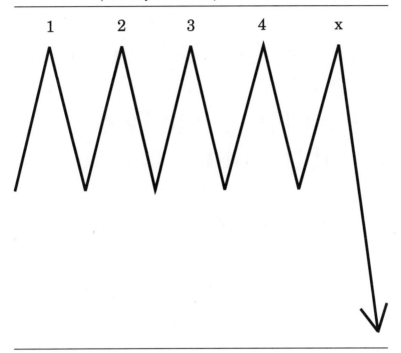

RULE 27

Dollar Cost Averaging Works Best with Stocks That Fluctuate Widely; If the Stock Is Not Always in a Declining Trend, You Should Come Out Ahead

The concept is based on frequently and consistently acquiring a stock over the life of an investment program with a fixed amount of capital each time. If you implement the plan, you buy a fixed dollar amount of stock, let's say $1,000 worth of IBM stock every month for the next 20 years. Over the life of the program you would have had the opportunity to pick up the stock at high prices and at low prices. At high prices you buy fewer shares, as it should be, and at lower prices you buy more shares, as it should be.

Figure 27.1 shows an example of dollar cost averaging at work. Note how the price of the particular stock in this example moves in two swings: one upward from $10 to $50, and one downward from $40 to $10. When the

FIGURE 27.1 Example of dollar cost averaging

Stock's Price at End of Month	Invest $1,000 Each Month	Cumulative Stock Position	Total Out of Pocket Cost	Cumulative Market Value	Profit or Loss
$10	100 shares	100 shares	$ 1,000	$ 1,000.00	$ 0.00
15	66.67 shares	166.67	2,000	2,500.00	500.00
25	40 shares	206.67	3,000	5,166.75	2,166.75
30	33.33	240	4,000	7,200.00	3,200.00
35	28.57	268.57	5,000	9399.99	4,399.99
40	25	293.57	6,000	11,742.80	5,742.80
35	28.57	322.14	7,000	11,274.90	4,274.90
30	33.33	355.47	8,000	10,664.10	2,664.10
25	40	395.47	9,000	9,886.75	886.75
15	66.67	462.14	10,000	6,932.10	-3067.90
10	100	562.14	11,000	5,621.40	-5,378.60

price moves upward, the profits are continual, but when the stock starts to move down the profits diminish rapidly and eventually the investor winds up holding positions with an average price considerably higher than the current market price. At the last addition of $10 for the 100 shares, the average price of the total position, before the final addition is 462.14 shares with $10,000 invested, or an average price of $21.64 per share. After the addition of the 100 shares at $10, the total position is now $562.14 for an average price of $19.56. So, the investor has managed to reduce his or her average position's price by $21.64 minus $19.56, or $2.07 a share. Looking at this another way, the investor put up another $1,000 to reduce his total position's cost by $2.07 a share. Is this good or bad? Neither since this approach takes a long-term perspective. Implied is the belief that when the stock dips down to $10 the second time around the price will eventually go back up, beyond the now average position price of $19.56. It violates a lot of trading rules and strategies, such as "never add to a losing position and put stop orders to protect profits," but the reader can implement these rules and strategies personally into this dollar cost averaging scenario and improve the plan tremendously.

This is a very basic approach and works well. However, it is also simplistic and negates the need to constantly monitor the fundamental and technical activities of the investment product. So, I have two suggestions to make this approach more effective.

First, find stocks that have a high probability of being around 20 years from now. These stocks are leaders in their industries and have a record over the last 20 years of expanding and paying out dividends. An ideal stock would be a growth stock that develops and then as it matures it takes its profits and proffers dividends to stockholders. You might want to consider this method for a core holding of stocks; this core holding makes up a good portion of your investment funds. Nothing is worse than owning a stock through the dollar cost averaging method and watching the stock go bankrupt.

The second point is to diversify your risk with this strategy by purchasing more than one company's stock. A reasonable number would be five quality stocks. With the fact that these companies are quality stocks, i.e., will be around 20 years from now, having five such companies will mitigate disastrous bankruptcies.

When diversifying in this program make sure the companies you have picked for your program are not interrelated. Dollar cost averaging a portfolio of five companies over the life of 20 years when these companies are centered in one industry is not diversifying. A good mix would be to pick a computer stock, telecommunication stock, transportation stock, food stock, and entertainment stock.

Each of these industries move in different bottoming and topping cycles. They don't have correlated cycles. When one is up the others will be down. With the one that's up, you buy less stock; with the one that's down, you buy more stock. With the paper profits on the one that's up, you offset the paper losses on the ones that are down.

Over the life of this program you will create a portfolio of stocks which will pay out a good dividend and will continue to grow. A subtler benefit of this approach is that this is a forced savings plan with the savings going into a stable group of stocks.

RULE 28

Analyze Your Strong Points and Convert Them into Even Stronger Ones

As a trader, always know your strong and weak points. Can you make the distinction between the two so that you can concentrate on developing the strong points and mitigating the impact of the weak points?

What may be my strong points might be your weak points, vice versa. You won't know what your weak points are until you continually get yourself into trouble whenever these weak points are around. The strong points aren't the ones we worry about, but these non-troublesome points can't be really strong points until you work on developing them to be strong points. The weak points are flaws in your makeup which prevent you from succeeding in the trading business.

For a vast majority of traders, successful or not, the problem of overtrading is a weak point. Few traders have enough discipline to measure risk—a strong point—and limit market exposure by deliberate undertrading (which is neither a strong point nor a weak point). Another common weak point is our desire to trade only one market, or to the other extreme, trade in many markets. Both are weak points because they don't help you to address the correct way to diversify risk.

What are the strong points? Are the strong points the antitheses of the weak points? Is the opposite of overtrading, a weak point, the trading of a few contracts, a strong point? From a logical perspective, yes, but from the perspective of realistic application of successful trading strategies to the markets, they are not.

Unlike the polarity paradigm—strong points versus weak points—successful market trading requires development of strong points which are not derived from performing the opposite of weak points. Knowing what these areas are is only the start for the successful development of traders. The ongoing development of strong points will eventually make the trader successful.

To develop the strong point and overcome an overtrading problem, the reader cannot deliberately undertrade. To develop undertrading skills is not the development of a strong point. Undertrading to solve an overtrading problem is merely a mechanical way to eliminate an overtrading problem; this is not the development of a strong point. However, to eliminate overtrading successful traders must find a strong point to work on that is totally removed from the overtrading-undertrading polarity: develop your skills to measure market risk! By developing this skill, you will understand why you overtraded when you shouldn't have. You might discover that you weren't aware of how much more capital you needed to take on another ten contracts. You might discover that you weren't sure of how grain futures negatively or positively correlated with financial futures and because of this you doubled up on market risk by selling the grains and buying the financials. Thus you will have strengthened a skill, not simply have done the opposite of overtrading to compensate for an overtrading problem.

We as traders have such a hard time trying to figure out what we must do to succeed in the markets. We think that to do the opposite of what we have been doing wrong is to act on a strong point. Not so. To act in an opposite way is merely to respond negatively to wrongful action. This is not the development of strong points!

Your strong points should also be positive attributes, not negative ones. Positive attributes are those that you can strengthen. You can never strengthen a response to a negative action! In a sense, when you entrench yourself in strengthening a response to a negative action you will be actually strengthening the negative action! Let's say you're playing with matches and get burned. The act of getting burned is a negative action. You hurt yourself. The response to this negative action is not to play with matches. You can live out the rest of your life not getting anywhere near to matches, but this would limit you in your understanding of many things related to fire: heat, energy, light, etc., in short all the benefits of being able to use fire constructively. You can stay away from a match for a long time. Instead, you can find a positive strong point which you can develop and strengthen; this positive strong point might be something as simple as studying and using fire constructively so that you can take advantage of the next set of matches that comes your way. This is a positive strong point which you can develop, and in the process, eliminate the negative action of getting burned. There is no guarantee that you won't ever get burnt in the future, but more benefits will accrue to you.

So instead of undertrading, find a strong point which you can develop which will eliminate the problem of overtrading. My suggestion is to develop your ability to measure risk. You might find another solution which is uniquely your own to deal with the problem of overtrading.

One of the benefits of developing positive strengths is that these will change your behavior for longer time periods. Responses to negative actions are temporary and fleeting. Once the negative actions are removed we fall quickly back into the same old defeating behavior patterns. This is because of the element of expediency. If you are reprimanding your child you will get your quickest result in altering his behavior with the threat of a negative: beating the child. This is *not* the longest-lasting way to behavioral change, however. If you take the time to praise your child when he or she does behave well you will obtain the longest-lasting change in behaviors; however, you have to invest time and effort to notice and praise your child's good behavior. The same goes with the markets. You must spend time to find the positive strong points to strengthen and even more time in cultivating the strengths.

Learning to trade involves many negative forces, not positive ones, but developing the positive forces will make you a successful trader.

RULE 29

There Is No Room in the Marketplace for Generosity or Sentiment

I remember the first stock I ever bought, Benrus Corporation, a maker of watches, and I saw the value of my stock holding disappear to nothing.

I was a stock trader trainee at a Third market trading operation in 1971. After spending several months on the training desk to be a company trader I read an article in *Business Week* magazine about the turnaround situation at Benrus Corporation. The stock was trading around $10⅝ considerably off the lows of about $2½. I had $500 in savings, so I bought 50 shares at the high of the move. I got caught up in the emotional fervor flamed by the bullishness of the article.

I paid $10⅝, the highest price the stock ever saw before it went bankrupt years later. And I was naive enough to mention to the other eight company traders that I bought the stock based on a bullish article in *Business Week*.

All during those years I held onto the stock because I thought it would go up. I also held it because the people in my trading office laughed at me when I bought the odd lot. I held it because I became emotionally attached to it.

It wasn't exactly like the headline in one of the most successful advertisements ever created: "I Sat Down at the Piano and They All Laughed till I Played." It was more like: "I Sat Down at the Desk and Told Them I Bought Benrus and They Have Been Laughing Ever Since."

I still have the stock certificate. I framed it several years after I bought the. stock to serve as a reminder of my stupidity. Several relatively inexpensive lessons I learned from this debacle eventually saved me hundreds of thousands of dollars as my trading career progressed.

Stocks and commodities are not human and you can sell them without feeling guilt or remorse. They are objects of possession. The only reason you acquire these assets is to sell them at higher prices. No matter how much the marketing forces try to personify these assets, they are not human. One of the best ways to market stocks is to personify them, i.e., imbue human qualities into them. Use emotions tugging words such as: "widow and orphans stock" for AT&T or IBM. In the process of selling stock to the buying public, marketers create personal stories to increase the chances that these marketed stocks will be able to compete with newer issues coming out on the open market. This correlates well with the old marketing adage that people usually buy to satisfy emotional needs and justify their buying decision after their purchase.

If you purchase a company's stock or a commodity and refuse to sell it in the face of losses because of sentimental reasons, i.e., human reasons, then I would suggest that you stay away from this area of capital accumulation and consider investing in something as emotional as real estate. You should, for example, buy the AT&T stock for your nephew or niece because you think the stock is fundamentally very good, not because your niece or nephew needs dividends to pay for an operation or pay college tuition. If you buy a stock or commodity, you also have to recognize when to sell it, especially if you discover that you made a mistake and you see that you have no way to make a profit: Cut your losses.

Every time I am tempted to make a stupid investing decision based on emotion, all I have to do is look up on my wall to see the worthless Benrus stock certificate hanging up there and then turn my attention elsewhere. A cheap lesson that has saved me hundreds of thousands of dollars. Humiliating, but cheap.

RULE 30

Stocks Need Sponsors To Bolster Their Prices; Stocks Do Not Go Up by Themselves

No stock has ever gone up by itself. However, stocks have come down without any support.

Over the course of the years watching and monitoring stocks I've come to the conclusion that you can find ways to discover how one company is dealing with another company. This information is available throughout the information distribution channels, but you have to know what and where to look for them. The following details of a company-sponsored investment campaign will show you what some of these telltale clues are.

Let me relate an intriguing story to you about my own experiences with Hughes Tools stock which I tracked and monitored over the course of several years. Spanning several years, this example illustrates the dealings that go on all the time in the marketing of stock. This chapter details the acquisition, marketing, and apparent distribution of a company stock by another company.

The company was privately held. Its ancestral heritage is based on the fact that Howard Hughes's father created this company in 1909. On December 7, 1972, it went public with hardly any fanfare. On January 28, 1987, 15 years later Baker International Corporation combined with Hughes Tools and the companies are now known as Baker Hughes International.

Among the many companies supporting the upward price move was a company called Borg Warner, which later bought back its own stock and became a privately held company. Borg Warner, now privately held, spun off two Borg Warner divisions: Borg Warner Security and Borg Warner Automotive. Borg Warner Security Corporation meanwhile has seen earnings drop precipitously. Borg Warner Automotive was spun off from Borg Warner Corporation in 1993. In October 1994, it held a second stock offering that raised more than $66 million to fund company operations. Recently the price of these stocks has dropped tremendously. Draw your own conclusions. As a private company it no longer has to disclose its finances to the public.

Before Borg Warner became a privately held company, I became interested in Hughes Tool stock. However, I didn't know the link between the two companies till I was pretty heavily involved trading Hughes Tool stock for my market-maker account at the Chicago Board Options Exchange about 15 years ago.

Beefing Up Hughes Tool Stock After Positioning the Stock

According to the Hughes Tool annual statement, Borg Warner sold one of its divisions, Byron-Jackson, to Hughes Tools in October 1974; Borg Warner received 500,000 shares of $6.25 cumulative convertible preferred stock in Hughes Tools. The conversion rate was 7.5 shares of common for each preferred.

The investment in the Hughes's stock was carried at net book value of the Byron Jackson operations at the effective date of the transaction and is reflected in "non-current assets." (Borg Warner Annual Report, 1975).

Several years later, Borg Warner sold Centrilift to Hughes Tools for additional stock, but this time it was straight common stock, not cumulative preferred. In Borg Warner's 1979 Annual Report, Chairman Bere of Borg Warner was asked why it sold Centrilift to Hughes Tool for stock. In the process of explaining this, he also disclosed why Borg Warner sold its Byron-Jackson operations to Hughes Tool:

"A bit of background might help explain our reason. Borg Warner already owned 3.75 millions shares of Hughes's common stock in exchange for our oil well service operations in 1974. This has proved to be a very successful transaction for both companies. Because the sharply focused nature of Hughes Tool closely matched that of the unit we sold them, that unit has grown and prospered to a greater degree as part of Hughes than would probably have been the case had it remained part of Borg Warner. In exchange, our investment in the form of Hughes stock has proved a very satisfactory one for Borg Warner shareholders. We expect the same will be true of Centrilift. The additional 1.2 million shares of Hughes Tool common stock we would receive would give Borg Warner slightly more than 20 percent of Hughes Tool stock outstanding. This would permit us to include that share of Hughes' profits in our future earnings. Because of the future growth we expect for both Centrilift and Hughes, we believe the transaction will allow Borg Warner shareholders to participate more fully in the vital energy market." (Borg Warner 1979 Annual Report)

This statement shows that Borg Warner was deliberately beefing up Hughes Tools earning prospect. So the positioning stage of Hughes Tool stock started as early as 1974, possibly earlier than 1972 when the company became public. This stage was brilliantly executed: Borg Warner got paid to hold stock in Hughes Tool in the form of a cumulative preferred. With the cumulative preferred, Borg Warner was getting paid the going market interest rate to hold Hughes Tool Stock. I've discovered when the insiders play in the marketplace, they make sure all costs are covered. And the preferred was convertible to stock.

Value Is Discovered and the Price Moves Up

Bere had admitted that his company, Borg Warner, had positioned in Hughes Tool. Then he disclosed that the next acquisition by Hughes Tool of Borg Warner's Centrilift division would also be beneficial to Hughes Tools.

Hughes Tool paid Borg Warner 1,200,000 shares of Hughes's stock for Borg Warner's Centrilift. In the process of doing so, Borg Warner now owned close to over 20 percent of Hughes Tool. The accounting procedures kicked in: Borg Warner now could incorporate the earnings of their holdings in Hughes Tool into Borg Warner's earnings statement. Overnight, Borg Warner which had been holding Hughes Tool stock in the form of non earning assets, now had assets which were earning as much as Hughes Tool stock showed . . . earnings from which Borg Warner's formerly owned division, Byron-Jackson, and now formerly owned Centrilift, contributed to Hughes Tool!

James Bere became Borg Warner's Chairman of the Board and Chief Executive Officer in 1972. In 1974, Bere became a director of Hughes Tool. A year later, in 1975, Raymond M. Holliday, the Chief Executive Officer of Hughes Tool since the company became public in

1972, became a director at Borg Warner! Cross director-ships! Some interesting things were about to happen.

Telltale Clues Forecast a Price Move

I started to monitor the stock when I became a member of the Midwest Stock Exchange's Options market. At the time that I was tracking the unfolding of the eventual runup of Hughes Tool stock, I was applying the on-balance-volume (OBV) technique developed by Joseph Granville. I became a devoted subscriber to his service for several reasons: He developed the accumulation indicator and he was getting a lot of press at the time. It was strictly out of a defensive posture that I needed to know what his thoughts on the markets were.

I was also using another technique, the Elliott Wave theory developed by Ralph Elliott in the early 1930s and currently espoused by Robert Prechter.

The stock had been trading in a tight range for several years. Granville published listings of stocks that he was bullish on in his newsletter. One issue placed Hughes Tools as a recommended buy. However, since I was tracking stocks with OBV I applied it to Hughes Tool and it did not show up as a breakout to the upside. The price moved above the trading range—a clear breakout after years of base building. Puzzled by the lack of a buy signal using the OBV technique, I sent a letter, as a subscriber to Granville's newsletter, asking him whether or not my analyses of Hughes Tool using his OBV technique was correct. I received no reply from him.

Since I was also using Elliott Wave theory, my analysis of the stock showed that the current breakout away from the high range of $40–$42 projected to a market top of about $96 a share for Hughes Tool. I sent an inquiry to Robert Prechter of the *Elliott Wave Theory* newsletter. He promptly replied that he thought that the stock was bullish.

Meanwhile, as a young and unseasoned analyst, I told everyone to load up on Hughes Tool. Some did and some didn't.

The stock started to charge up. As an experienced tape reader I noticed the bid and offers of the New York Stock Exchange specialist on the stock. It was being marked up. There was support coming into the stock because the bid and ask would show up a majority of the time with more stock being bid for than stock offered. The downticks would occur on 100 shares. Occasionally, there would be downticks of 500 shares. The upticks occurred on 1,000 shares or more. The upticks sometimes occurred on 5,000 shares blocks also. This indicated accumulation.

I watched the stock being marked up. It went up to $45 a share, rested and then moved up to the high 40s. If you were to go back to find a chart of the stock you would not be able to discern that the stock traded at $40–$45 per share around this time period because the past has already been obliterated and rewritten, with the use of several stock splits. The stock splits rewrote the highs and lows. See Chapter 17 on Sherwin-Williams for more details on this subtle but important point.

An Insider but A Peripheral Player: The Stock Specialist

Shortly after I started monitoring the stock I traveled to New York on business. I was clearing at Goldberg Securities at the time and I asked the clerks and floor personnel of the company whether or not they could show me the New York exchange floor when I got to New York. I wanted to speak to the specialist of Hughes Tool. As a naive observer I thought I would congratulate him on his ability to mark up the stock.

When I arrived at the exchange Goldberg assigned a runner to show me around the exchange. I asked the runner to show me the Hughes Tool's specialist post. The runner remarked that the specialist was one of the oldest ones there, and he didn't even know if the guy was still around. However, this did not prevent me from wanting to see where the stock was traded. I likened myself to a tourist visiting in a new city. I wanted to see the sights that were of interest to me.

As I rounded the corner of the specialist post the runner pointed out the specialist to me. I saw a congenial old man, with gray skin and a bald head. He wore a withered suit coat and was fiddling around with the orders placed in the slots in front of him. He reminded me a bit of the clerk Anderson from my first *Trading Rules* book. This was before the days of electronic trading so everything was still done manually.

The runner went up to the specialist and motioned for me to move closer. I was introduced as a trader from the Chicago Board Options exchange floor. We shook hands, and as I stood on the outside of the trading post watching the specialist, he engaged me in conversation.

I told him I thought he was brilliant in helping mark up the stock. He looked at me cautiously, saying nothing. Then I told him that I was a market-maker in Hughes Tool stock at the Chicago Board Options Exchange. This served to make me a member of the "club," an insider, too, if you will.

We discussed the stock a bit more, what I saw as the breakout and how I thought he was doing a skillful job of moving the stock up by tightening the bids and sloppily making the offers.

What then happened was unusual. The specialist motioned me to come over to his side of the post. He asked if I wanted to see his book of orders to buy and sell Hughes Tool. Of course I wanted to see it! What person who is involved in the markets wouldn't? As I moved into the post I saw in his eye a glint of "I'm going to show you something but you keep it under your hat" tone.

Then he showed me his book, which had about five orders, two on the buy side and three on the sell side, all several points away from the last sale. I cocked my head in amazement and asked the specialist what had happened to all the other orders. When I was market-making at the Chicago Board Options Exchange, I had noticed large buy and sell orders. There were always bids and asks from the specialist. He said there weren't any other orders. I asked him why there were so few in the book when I saw hundreds of thousands of shares trade daily on the stock. The orders must be there. He wasn't showing them to me.

He replied, "No. These are all the orders I have in my book. But let me tell you this, Bill (for by now we were on a first name basis), this is what I do: when the public comes in with orders to buy I sell them stock; when the public comes in to sell I buy the stock from them. This is all I do." When he told me this I observed a twinkle in his eye. First a glint, now a twinkle. I was now convinced that he treated me as a comrade . . . a comrade in arms.

I couldn't understand what he was telling me until months later back in Chicago as I watched Hughes Tool pop up close to $98 a share. The public and institutions were buying the stock all the way up. The orders I saw in the specialist's book were legitimately there, but other orders held by other brokers were never placed in the book. I would guess a good 90 percent of all orders existent at any time are not entered into a specialist's book.

The specialist, however, knew exactly where those orders were and who was holding them. At any time that he needed stock he could call these brokers to execute the orders, the specialist being the buyer of the stock. So, even though I only saw a few orders there were many, many orders that no one, except the specialist and the brokers holding the orders, knew existed.

Because of the specialist's privileged status he could match the orders. It was how business was conducted at the NYSE. The broker made his commissions when the specialists called the broker over to take the broker out of his orders.

In the meantime I saw the specialist put up bids and offers which gave me the impression as an outside floor trader that lots and lots of orders were bought and sold.

Although there were lots of orders to buy and sell, all were in the specialist's head, which could easily be "forgotten" or "remembered." This was all for the benefit of the specialist because the specialist could work his own markets closer or further away from the public orders.

There is no ethical issue here. It's neither right nor wrong for the specialist to be doing what he was doing. It's an accepted fact that that is how the game is played. Everybody in this business must follow the unwritten rules of profit-making. It's as simple as that.

Stock Price Moves Up

Meanwhile, the stock charged to new highs every week. I was happy because I was playing the stock from the long side. As the Hughes Tool scenario unfolded I began to sense more and more that I was a minute cog in the well-oiled machinery of stock distribution. It was one of the most impressive stock price moves I had ever seen in my twenty years of market observations; I have neither seen nor heard about anyone else writing or discussing this story. However, a trader can learn much from it. All the support personnel have since made their millions and left the game.

This was happening between the last half of 1979 and early 1980.

Two other players entered the fray. One major player was Borg Warner. A second, albeit minor, player was Baker International.

I noticed one day that Hughes Tool was buying a French oil drilling company. Hughes was on a roll and needed more drilling capacity. Imbedded in Hughes Tool 1979 Annual Report was this obscure note:

"In October 1979, the Company (Hughes Tool) acquired 90 percent of the stock of a subsidiary of Creusot-Loire for about $13,000,000. Beginning in 1980, the Company will use the two manufacturing plants acquired to manufacture rock bits and tool joints in France." (Note 2, page 33 of Hughes Tool 1979 Annual Report)

I thought it strange that out of nowhere appeared this obscure French company. The annual report did not mention it anywhere else by name. Elsewhere in the report, the company was always referred to as "a French company."

The French company was owned by Borg Warner. This was the first time I noticed that Borg Warner was involved, so I did more research. Borg Warner sold the company to Hughes Tool, the very company Borg Warner had stock interests in!

Thank goodness for the unseen, but free hand of market forces.

What I discovered later threw me for a loop. Hughes Tools raised money for itself by selling stock to the public. Among the many issues outstanding it had common stock and preferred stock. I found that only one company owned the preferred stock, namely Borg Warner. And this was a direct result of Borg Warner selling its companies, either named as Centrilift or the "Byron Jackson operations." Aha! The trail gets hotter.

Mind you, now, this was all information I got through publicly available channels. None of this information was secured. Yet, by tracking this one stock I found correlations and connections that the average investor would never have found! Unlike a lawyer in a court of law all I needed as a tape reader to draw my conclusions was circumstantial evidence. This is how most of the world operates. The hunter follows the bear tracks in the snow to find where the bear is. I saw my own "tracks." And they were indeed very fresh ones.

I positively concluded that Borg Warner had more than a passing interest in Hughes Tool. As the only preferred stockholder, it could ask for concessions and privileges others couldn't ask for nor get.

The questions in my mind evolved into, "If this is a price move then there has to be a distribution of stock somewhere in the upper 90s price projection I had in store for it. What would happen to get stock distributed at this level? A new stock offering? A merger with Hughes Tool stock as partial or complete payment? What could it possibly be?" I didn't know who was involved. I was dealing only with what information I had.

The Finale with a Coup de Grâce

At this time, the debt market was heating up also. Market interest rates were going up. They were at very high levels. So, what did the people at Hughes Tool do? They offered convertible debentures to raise cash.

I couldn't figure out why they offered to sell debentures and possibly lock themselves into long-term commitments to pay high interest rates. Why couldn't they wait till the debt market had settled down? Why do it now? The marketers, whoever they were, created and sold products when the public wanted them. They created a product which investors wanted: high interest bonds with a play on upward stock price movements! A two-pronged appeal to increase the number of investors and speculators. Stop for a moment to think about what was done. Instead of considering that they were giving up the shop, they literally gave away the shop. I was really puzzled with this. Where was the protection from losing control of their company?

In April 1980, Hughes Tool sold $100,000,000 worth of 8.5 percent Convertible Debentures, *callable* and convertible to 1,602,883 shares of common stock. This was their protection. The convertible debentures were callable at the company's discretion. Before the year was up the stock had traded above conversion and, you guessed it, the convertible debentures were called.

The last step made me sit up and take notice. The Hughes Tool people offered debentures at high interest rates—the buyers bought this offering like crazy. As a kicker they made the debentures convertible to Hughes Tool common stock. Now, the debenture owner could have a guaranteed rate of return and also take advantage of any possible capital gains on the underlying stock. What finesse! What smoothness!

But still this did not answer the question of how stock was going to be presented to the public. Price moves such as these are worth nothing and are ineffective if you aren't able to unload stock at higher prices.

(The Hunt brothers implemented a patently illegal and more drastic attempt. This is something that they did not do when they attempted to corner the sliver and gold markets. They accumulated the metals by laying their groundwork for acquisition, but they never laid the groundwork for distributing the precious metals they bought until it was too late. Their distribution stage was too late for them. Marc Rich, the notorious oil and metal trader, however, was careful in creating an infrastructure to distribute all the metals and oil that he bought and marked up. In the recent copper corner he was totally vertically integrated: he bought the mines, he bought the marketing companies, and he bought the refineries. In doing so he unloaded copper all the way through the various distribution channels!)

Hughes Tool offered the convertible debentures to the public. But they placed a string on their brilliant offer: they made the debentures callable by the company. That is, the company could call in the debentures at any time and pay the full maturity value for the debentures. This was an excellent strategy. If the debentures were sold and interest rates were expected to go up, then the original buyers of the debentures would be sitting with mark-to-market losses since the value of the bonds would have to go down to reflect the higher market interest rates. If the company then called the bonds in the company would be artificially forcing the price of the bonds back to maturity value. What a great bonus to the convertible debentures buyers; these buyers had a hybrid put in place.

The price of the stock continued to chug on up. It traded above the conversion ratio. At this point it made sense to convert the debentures into stock and sell the stock on the open market and make a profit. The debentures had appreciated in value and now traded above their maturity value. Not because of the interest rates, but because the underlying stock.

After Hughes Tool announced they were forcing the conversion, all debenture holders had to convert their bonds to stock unless, of course, the debenture holders sold the bonds in the open market or back to the company for maturity value.

In one fell swoop, the money owed by the company to the bond holders had now been reclassified as shareholder equity, which took away the credit rights that they had enjoyed as bondholders. In one fell swoop, the IOU of the company to the bondholders had been converted to equity interests which had no effective block voting power. In Hughes Tool's 1980 Annual Report, the note under Capital Stock read "The net proceeds from these transactions were credited to common stock and paid-in capital." As long as the stock stayed above the conversion ratio, former debentures holders now holding the stock would not want to sell because then they would have to realize capital gains. Another way to make sure the investors kept their money in the stock!

Hughes Tool then announced another stock split. The company had split before. In the process of splitting and offering additional treasury stock, Hughes Tool had made sure the increasing stock position that Borg Warner held in Hughes Tool would never be larger than 21 percent of total shares outstanding. While the 79 percent that was held by the public got increasingly larger in numbers of shares, the depreciating holdings of Hughes Tool by Borg Warner was more than offset by the money Borg Warner made on buying and selling produces and services to Hughes Tool.

What brilliance. What acumen. I really wanted to get in touch with some of these guys in management. I was absolutely awed and amazed.

Drawing Conclusions on a Stock Cycle

This was the end of the price move for Hughes Tool. Over the years I've watched the stock fall to the low teens. In April 1987, Hughes Tool merged with Baker International, to form Baker Hughes Inc. In the mid-1980s, Borg Warner acquired all the assets of Baker Industries, not to be confused with Baker International. But by this time I had learned enough of what power and force a concerted effort by moneyed interests can effectively do in the markets by using the right tools developed for the stock market to make similar plays.

Other companies and other stocks have gone through this with even more planning and finesse. Sponsorship exists even today just as it did around the turn of the century, when the bulk of sponsorship rested with the market movers. The process of accumulation and distribution will always be with us. In this example, I saw and related to the reader the symbiotic relationship between two companies: one willing to invest its cash and assets and another company which welcomed the investments.

RULE 31

Whatever Is Hard To Do in the Market Is Generally the Right Thing; Whatever Is Easy Is Usually the Wrong Thing To Do

As a trading strategy this rule doesn't mean a darn thing. As a valid observation of your interaction with the markets you'll find this to be true.

I happened upon this by accident one day while I was scalping in the pits. People always taught me that when bidding I should always bid under the last sale. When offering I should always offer over the last sale. This downtick or uptick is considered the "edge" in the scalping business. By securing the edge every time I made a trade, I had that extra tick as a comfort margin; I could take a tick loss on the next trade and come out even for two trades. In this manner scalpers have a decided advantage over others because they bid and offer at the market price which they make.

Well, I did exactly this and discovered that it was nearly impossible to bid for something under the last sale and get filled. The same with offering over the last sale. I seldom got filled because everybody else in the pit was trying to do the same. Those who were able to get filled worked a lot harder than me to get the trades. These scalpers were able to do this day in and day out. As a result of being able to get the edge these scalpers make a very good living. As far as I was concerned this was a lot of work.

Sometimes I did get filled on my bid or my offers. When I did get hit on the bid, the market dropped even more. The same happened when I got taken out on my offers. The market always ran higher. At times when my bids were hit and my offers were taken, the market was always running away from me.

This was always the case with me because I never fought for the trades and as a result I never really "won" any trades. All the trades that I "won," or to be more correct, those that filled at my prices were essentially given to me by other traders or brokers. In other words, I was essentially the trader left holding the bag all the time.

However, whenever I fought in the pits for the trades with the other traders, I wound up with trades that were eventually profitable, or at least trades which gave me a one-tick profit cushion for the next trade.

As a younger man I scalped like this in the pits and did well. As I got older this amounted to quite a bit of work. The knees gave way. Standing in the pits, fighting with the younger crowds, and scalping for ticks every day for hundreds of trades, turned into a chore.

When I never got hit on my bid or taken out on my offer I was really working the other side of the public orders. It was similar to the way I negotiated buying a car. When the seller agreed to my bid price I would then lower my price just a bit more so that no transaction actually occurred. When I eventually did make a low enough offer and the seller sold the car to me in frustration, I was assured that I had bought the car at the cheapest price, thus guaranteeing a profit! Buying a car in this manner was hard work, but I also knew it would never get me into trouble.

The same situation exists with trading the markets. If I continually lowered my bid when trying to buy I would buy at the lowest price and ensure that I would be able to sell it at a profit or at least get the same price I bought it for.

But when I was more lax and did not want to continually play this cat and mouse game I would get my bid filled rather quickly. In these times I knew that the positions I had acquired didn't have much chance of being profitable. This would further depress prices and I wouldn't have a chance to unload what I had accumulated. The easy thing always got me into trouble and it always had me long on a breakdown and short in a rally!

The only way I managed to make money doing this was to continue doing it but also be aware of runners coming into the pits with orders in their hands. I would immediately jump into the fray and bid under and offer over, hoping that I would be one of the first in line to get the orders. This was really work!

As my trading progressed to longer-term position trading I noticed the same thing happening with research reports that I was trying to secure. I noticed the harder it was for me to get information on any stock or commodity the more often it looked like profitable situations. You only have to look at the Hughes Tool in Chapter 30 to know that following a stock like this for several years takes time and effort—it is hard to do.

The easier it was for me to get the research reports, the greater the chance that the rest of the world would have known about these profitable plays. As a result, the plays wound up being less profitable. This is why I really seldom subscribe to the investment letters written by the well-known market gurus. Everybody else knows about those plays. Give me some of those obscure writers whose analytical skills far surpass their marketing skills and I'll find a way to make money with that information.

Here's another example which might be closer to home: When working their leads for new business, excellent salespeople tell me they jump for joy when they get prospects who are difficult to reach for legitimate reasons such as doctors or lawyers who are busy all the time. These are the prospective clients you specifically want to go after; since no other salesperson has been able to reach them, the one persistent salesperson who does reach these prospects has a much higher chance of acquiring these prospects as accounts.

So when you see a situation which looks like an easy lay-up, don't really pin your career on it—it may not be as profitable as you think, and may not last long enough for you to build a career. But if you see a trading situation that requires investments of blood, sweat and tears—push a little harder for you will have a better chance of success.

RULE 32

A Reaction in a Bull Market and a Decline in a Bear Market Are Not One and the Same

To this I must also add the inverse: A rally in a bear market and an upmove in a bull market are not one and the same.

I watch market commentators on television and listen to them on radio all the time. As a trader, you have to sort out and interpret the massive amounts of information very carefully.

One major flaw with much of the media commentary is misreading the markets. Many commentators don't know whether they are reporting on market conditions in bear markets or bull markets. So many of them tend to view the markets as bullish. If they don't know the stage of the market cycle they are in, their interpretations of bull markets and their reactions as well as bear markets and their reactions can mislead a lot of viewers and listeners.

Another more basic reason why these commentators are inclined to always view the markets in bullish terms is based on the inclination of the public to be bullish most of the time. A market commentator must talk to an audience who has built-in bull market filters. Talking about down markets to this audience will be a wasted effort. They won't heed the comments; they will do what they want.

What can a market commentator do? Do commentators pander to the public's desire for bullish scenarios all the time, or do the commentators talk about the bearish scenarios, too? From my own experience, whether you are a market commentator or a trader, it's always best to be an objective observer of the market condition. Always try to observe and report truth.

If you faithfully observe the truth, all your strategies and trading decisions revolving around that sound core of observation are sound. If you create strategies and decisions based on fallacy, you will have to justify and reinterpret reality continually to keep propping up the facade of truth. In the markets you will end up wasting valuable time and money if you continue to misperceive market dictated realities. Here are reminders of what you must not do:

- Don't keep adding more money to a losing position.
- Don't switch to brokers who agree with you all the time; you need a balanced perspective of the markets, not a perspective which is strictly your own.
- Don't continue to trade stocks which never make profits for you.
- Don't devise more complex and clever strategies to squeeze the last pennies out of a trade all the while ignoring the fact that profits from the markets come not from executions, but correct trading management.
- Don't keep grinding down the cost of executions expecting that maximizing profits in this area will insure profits.

- Don't keep spreading different markets against losing positions.
- Don't continue buying more complex hardware and software hoping that such expensive toys alone will make you a better trader, etc.

Below are all the primary trend movements and their corrective behaviors:

1. Reactions in bull markets are followed by a resumption of the bullish move.
2. Declines in bear markets are often followed by half-hearted rallies only to have the bear markets resume their downward move.
3. Rallies in bull markets are followed by mild selloffs and resume bullishly upwards.
4. Corrections in bear markets are followed by a resumption of selloffs.

The last two items take care of the flip side of the coin. I've covered all primary trend movements and their corrective behaviors.

Basic success in trading and investing in markets starts at one point: Correctly assess what market stage you are in. Are you in a bull market? Are you in a bear market? Or, are you in a trading market? If you are to extract profits from these markets you must apply the correct methods to trading these markets. If you incorrectly assess your market stage, your trading decisions will be flawed. They will be flawed not because the trading decisions are in themselves bad, but because the *premise upon which you apply these decisions is incorrect.* Most readers instead blame the trading decisions as being bad.

Start correctly, or don't start at all. Once you start, then execute well.

RULE 33

The Three Key Words for Successful Long-Term Investment and Reducing Risk Are 1) Management, 2) Management, 3) Management

No stock is completely safe; ownership in any stock has some element of risk. All investments have risk; let's evaluate why there are risks. What does ownership of a stock of a company really entail?

The only situation which entails no risk involves complete inertia: death. Aside from this one example every market situation that you look at contains an element of risk; the markets are in constant flux, responding to stimuli and also acting as a catalyst for other situations. The wise trader or investor can evaluate the validity of those risks considerably in advance. Without risk, you won't be able to make much profit, and inflation will eat away at your savings. However, you must evaluate and manage risk if you are going to profit from it.

Let's discuss the element of humanness. Despite the fact that stocks are objects, the human mind has created them.

All stocks begin by being owned by the companies that created them. Companies then issue shareholder interests in the form of stock.

These companies' objectives are to maximize their resources for the benefit of first its management, then employees, and then investing shareholders. Let's admit it: as a shareholder, you're last in line to benefit. Management and workers have first priority on all profits. Anything left trickles down to the investors.

However, why do some companies tell us they will have record earnings and the earnings reports turn up flat? A company will deny being interested in buying another company and the next day the announcement of a buyout is made? Or, a company tells us the sale of their assets are in the best interest of the shareholders and years later you find out company assets have been diverted to a holding company? Well, they do not set out to deceive us; it's simply that companies have different agendas, which may or may not match our own.

The company management can choose from so many ways to reward the management themselves and the investors. For example, they might want to take all the profits and plow them back into the company to increase future profits. Thus, their record earnings may turn up flat. Or they might want to divvy everything up in the form of dividends. Or they might even do a bit of both by issuing stock dividends instead.

So, when you view the company, look *first* at the management. Don't forget about the worst case scenario, which is bad management. With bad management, there is no hope for a company or your investment in it. If you conclude that the company has bad management, avoid investing in it.

If you find a company with management that is centered around increasing the management's benefits, the investment scenario is better. But the company's primary objective is still not for the benefit of the shareholders. Shareholder benefits from this type of company management accrue accidentally and as a by-product of the company's success. The company's management can't help it if you, as a shareholder, see appreciation in their stock's price because they are doing a good job of keeping their jobs.

If you find a company with management centered completely around shareholder benefits, the scenario is excellent; but the chances of this occurring is slim to none. No company that I know of exists solely for the benefit of shareholders and I guarantee with a high degree of probability that no such company will be forthcoming for the next 100 years. Is this tragic? Not really, since you can't fault company management for taking care of itself first. Then everybody else falls next in line.

So keep in mind the three keywords for successful long-term investment: 1) Management; 2) Management; and 3) Management. Remember to look at company management closely.

RULE 34

Set Realistic Expectations of the Market; Do Not Anticipate More Than the Market Can Give—You Will Avoid Disappointment

A trader friend who is a member of one of the exchanges in Chicago discussed his new trading approach one day. He was on the migration path of moving his trading from working on the floor to trading off the floor; he was moving upstairs. *Upstairs* is a term used in the business to indicate that one is trading the markets in an office with computerized trading techniques.

He had developed a trading approach which took advantage of the Treasury bonds' futures contracts intermediate swings. A *swing* describes a chart pattern that is defined by a reasonable top followed by a reasonable bottom, or vice versa. (*The Technical Analysis of Stocks, Options & Futures,* explains swings in more detail.) If a market makes a high of 200 after bouncing off a low of 150, I consider the "swing" to be 50 points. The difficulty of defining what is a swing is based on your parameter for defining what the low is and what the high is. In addition to dealing with this subjective problem, you must also define from your own perspective whether or not the markets are bullish or bearish.

The explanation of a swing is critical to your understanding this chapter. Once a swing is defined accurately, the trader can determine what the maximum profit he or she could have attained had he or she traded it correctly. This is similar to saying that the high and low of a day's price action would have been the maximum amount of profits you could have attained had you bought the low and sold the high.

You also have to keep in mind that you can't squeeze blood out of a turnip even though many people try. A lot of traders try to squeeze the last tick out of a trade and don't realize they are doing that.

My trader friend had devised a trading market system which took advantage of the swings. The system enabled him to buy within 5 percent of a bottom and sell within 5 percent of a top. Unknown to him, however, this system only operated in trading markets. Operated in the sense that it was kicking out 100 percent profits annualized.

He traded the system for several months. He applied it to the bonds. After consistently making profits with the system he complained to me that his system wasn't making *enough* profits.

We sat down and talked about the system. At first, he was hesitant because he was fearful he would disclose something new to me. I assured him that if he gave me enough data points from his system I could recreate his system accurately. I know enough about the markets that I know what to look for in other people's systems and zero right in on those features.

Once assured he would not be telling me anything new, he opened up to me. His system had cranked out an average of three-quarters of a point profits in the Treasury bonds every time he entered a trade and closed a trade. His system basically allowed him to make money consistently in a trading range market. I said that was fine. The system was designed to do exactly that and it did that. I continued to ask him why he was displeased with it.

Since this trader was testing his system out with capital which was expected to be lost, he wanted the capital to last as long as possible: he only traded in one bond futures contract size. He did not want to increase the size of his positions.

So what was the problem I asked. He said he wanted to make 1½ points per trade and he was trying to redesign the system. I cautioned him that he couldn't extract blood from a turnip.

And suppose that he was able to extract blood from a turnip; what would he do with that type of "blood?" You can make sound money from profits in the markets. This type of money gives you a good feeling because you did everything right to get the profits. You deserve those profits. Windfall profits, money made because you happened to be there or just due to plain luck, always gnaw at you because you know you were not instrumental in getting the money. Because you had no direct control over making that money you have this fear that it can be taken away from you at any time. Fear, in any form and from any source, is a hard emotion to control.

Not so with money made solidly, with all the rules clicking exactly. That money is yours. It has your name on it. Instead of George Washington's picture on the money, your picture is on it.

I suggested that he continue using the system, but increase his trading size from one lot to two lots so he could make 1½ points per trade, not per contract. He declined, saying that the doubling of his position increased his market risk. I agreed with his analysis.

We continued discussing. We looked at the charts to try and figure out ways to squeeze an extra ¾ points out of the trade without increasing his risk commitment.

There was no known way he could get this to happen. Why? After further analyzing the chart patterns I discovered the average low to high and high to low swing was about 1 full point. His system was based on picking the swing high to sell and cover at the swing low or picking the swing low to buy and selling on the swing high. Since the swing themselves travelled about one point, there was no way he could have squeezed 1½ points. This was impossible.

In a sense, he was trying to tell me that water is not wet. That the sun doesn't shine. That the earth doesn't revolve around the sun. That with closed eyes he could see. What he wanted not only was unrealistic but also unattainable.

The discussion left me with a couple of conclusions: The market can only offer what it can offer. No matter how my friend tried to tamper with his system he could not extract another ½ point out of the system, without increasing his total number of contracts traded. The markets can give out only so much profit. To expect it to do more is foolish. The markets are not there for your profit. The markets are there because they're there. And you are there because you happen to be so. You must follow the market and go with the flow. If the market averages a 10-points-a-day move, to think that you can get it to move 15 points in one day because you need to make an extra five points is unrealistic.

This conclusion accounts for periods of feast and famine which is indigenous to the trading and investing business. There are times when money to be made in the business far exceeds the normal worker's income. There are also times when you can't find two nickels to spare from workers in the business.

This is an extremely fickle business.

As the trader considered his situation more, he slowly realized that what he wanted, and what the markets could offer him, were entirely two different things. So who ruled the day? The market or my trader friend?

As I wrote in *Trading Rules*, you should look for rates of returns from the markets which are better than average but not unrealistically high. In my friend's case, the market reality did not line up with his perceptions of the market; do not push the market for greater returns than can be normally expected. If the average rate of return is 10 percent per annum on a risk-free basis anything that offers better than that is something to consider. But do not expect rates of returns in the three-digit categories: 100 percent, 200 percent or 300 percent. These rates of returns require high risks of capital. If upon further investigation you discover that these high rates are valid, then these situations are specialized and most likely also temporary—the rest of the world hasn't discovered the investment strategy or vehicles yet. It's only a matter of time and then rates of returns will revert back to normal. High rates of returns in any area will draw attention and competition from other investment products and services. These rates will then drop as more competitive products come on board.

RULE 35

Define Market Action First, Then Take Appropriate Action

My trader friend, mentioned in the previous chapter, later complained to me that he had developed another trading system that no longer worked. He did not tell me whether it was a trading market system or a trending market system because he didn't know. Both systems are valid under certain conditions. He made money with his system continuously.

One day the copper market started a massively bullish move to the upside. He complained that his system got him short on the way up and he had to continually cover his shorts. As a result, he was going to throw out his trading system.

This trader, however, was unaware that he was applying a trading system to a market condition which had changed. If you could personify a trading system, he should have thanked it, instead of shunting it aside. He was going to throw out all his tedious research and look for some other method to trade.

By now it was apparent to me that he was really using a trading market system: he sold the highs and bought the lows. So I suggested that he take a look at his system again. Had he created a trending market system he would have taken long positions in anticipation of the bullish move. The copper market had become congested for a number of months, which accounts for the profits he had made with his trading market system.

The copper market now trended instead of traded. How could my friend, the trader expect a system, a static system at that, to adapt to a changed market condition? His actions and comments indicated that he had expected the system to modify itself for the newer conditions. Traders essentially take real-time data and constantly retrofit the data for constantly shifting parameters used in fixed formulas. Not only are you shooting at a moving target, you're also moving as you attempt to shoot the target!

As a matter of fact, all systems are static. They cannot adapt to new market conditions. Even the new strategies and techniques in vogue which have been recently developed around neural nets and artificial intelligence are static. Neural nets claim to take current market information and make forecasts with the most recent modified information; this is adaptive and not predictive. It's adaptive because it is still form and curve fitting brought closer, albeit, to real-time.

The trader agreed that he was actually using a trading market system! Before he continued on his path to discover the trending market system I suggested to him that, instead of throwing out the trading market system, he use the information given off by this system as a clue to other situations. The fact that he was losing money with a trading market system disclosed an important piece of information: those indications showed that he was no longer in a trading market!

214

Always look for the obvious and then read between the lines. The new information you garner can be as subtle as seeing the answers from a different perspective. By redefining the results of his trading market system in a new market condition which did not offer profits, he could easily confirm this was most likely a trending market.

He, therefore, had to change his approach. If he hadn't done this he would have forever been cursing the trading market system for having done him wrong, when in reality he was using a tool which couldn't be expected to perform under the new market conditions. Blame only those that are responsible, not those you think should be blamed. So keep in mind that certain approaches work in trading markets and some approaches are better suited for trending markets.

RULE 36

You Can Make Greater and More Rapid Profits in a Bull Market by Trading in Stocks of Small Capitalization, but *Watch Out* for the Risks

Although I have never used this rule, I have observed others who have done so successfully . . . and all by accident.

At this stage of the market cycle (mid-1995), I can say with a high probability that the long sustained bull move from 1982 is culminating. During the last two years we have seen more stocks trading in the over-the-counter (OTC) markets than ever before and initial public offerings (IPOs) snapped up by the investing public with hardly a thought on their investment qualities. Prices on some of these unseasoned, and unproven, stocks have shown virtually straight upward moves!

Around the end of 1992, for the whole year of 1993, and going into early 1994, a phenomenon occurred in tertiary stocks which I had never seen before, but which others familiar with the markets had probably observed. These stocks took off on their own and punched through new highs.

The public was suckered into buying the cats and dogs, the garbage stocks. "Cats and dogs" is a pejorative term for stocks which are at the bottom of the heap of investment quality. They are speculative. These can sometimes be new issues without a history of earnings or growth. Many of these OTC stocks and IPOs are not quality issues; these stocks hold the promise of further growth, but the majority of them will not be around in twenty or thirty years. The mutual funds representing the public also bought en masse.

Let's look at what happened to these stocks. What is amazing is that these small issue stocks shot up in price at the tailend of a bull market move. This complements particularly well the rule of this chapter: buy small cap stocks in bull markets to benefit from the upward biases. Successful traders know that many investors buy at the wrong time, and these traders use this information to make profits.

However, as I mentioned earlier, I have never used this rule. As a seasoned professional, instead of partaking in this final feasting, I took it as a signal that the bull market was rapidly aging. Instead of getting caught up in the bullish feverishness of these small cap stocks rushing to new highs at this market cycle, I stepped aside. When money managers create mutual funds that specialize in small cap stocks the writing on the wall says to me "Bull market ending. Beware." Small cap stocks are not stocks which can be counted on to remain bullish in bad economies. Small companies are always the first to feel the brunt of any recession in the general economy.

What about the possibility of shorting such stocks in bear markets? Can you short light capitalization stocks in bear markets and obtain the same quick profit making opportunities? The answer is not the reverse of the rule in this chapter. The next chapter will explore this question with a particular emphasis on trading activity which is the direct opposite of buying thin stocks in bull markets.

RULE 37

Liquid Stocks Can Be Covered More Expeditiously Than Small Caps

The chances for covering when trading short are better in a liquid stock with a large number of shares outstanding such as U.S. Steel, IBM, or Intel. Others with a small issue of shares may be more volatile and may jump a point or two between sales, thus hurting your chances to profit from trading short. So, do not short stocks with limited shares.

George Seamons, a noted writer of market books from the 1930s, observed there were different types of behavior attributable to different types of stocks in different types of markets. For example, the previous chapter showed that buying cheap small cap stocks at the tail-end of a bull market will show enormously high rates of profits. The converse, shorting cheap and small cap stocks, however, is not true; it will not necessarily give quick profits, but instead can leave the short holder vulnerable for counterposition rallies.

Let's analyze why. Keep in mind that in general markets which go up are not exact mirror images, both in form or function, of markets which go down.

One of my observations from professionally trading the markets for more than 20 years is that stocks and commodities must be "professionally" sponsored to go up (see Chapter 30 on Hughes Tools). If they are neglected, they will go down without much effort.

If you are looking for a stock to short, you want all the odds on your side, all the factors skewed for your benefit.

For example, when you pick a stock to short, you don't want a stock that will shoot up against you. Lightly traded stocks, such as cheap and small cap stocks, shoot to the moon when the buying frenzy heats up. This automatically eliminates thinly traded stocks, which can violently move once the public grabs hold of them. What does this leave you with? Stocks that are moderately traded and those that are actively traded. Of the two, you skew the odds even more in your favor by picking a volume active stock because you're trying to find situations in which not all the participants are fully aware of what is happening to their stocks most of the time.

The more players you have in this game, the greater your chances of getting the edge over one of them. Sheer numbers count even in this. Your objective is to move yourself into the category of winning traders and investors.

RULE 38

There Is No Substitute for Quality Experience in the Marketplace

Although there is no substitute for experience, a lot of people out there try to substitute sheer intensity for quality experience.

When I conduct seminars and workshops some attendees ask me what is the quickest way to make money in the markets. So I tell them about the systems and methods I have devised which are essentially no brainers but require a firm belief that the systems will continue to work.

Without much effort on their part these same people then start to ask details of the systems. Then it's only a matter of time when they ask "what-if" questions: what if I shortened the moving average, what if I looked at weekly charts, what if I compared it to another market, etc.

Essentially, all the questions asked are another way of asking this question:

What if it doesn't work?

We may want to get everything quick and fast, but when it comes time to put up money on these quick-and-dirty systems, these same people have gnawing doubts about applying a strict faith adherence to these methods.

What these people lack is the experience they intuitively feel must be applied to these systems over time. They know enough to realize that a system might work for me, but it won't work for them when they try to apply it. And, when it doesn't work for them, what can they do about it?

After conducting hundreds of seminars and workshops I've arrived at a satisfactory answer:

Then you will have to rely on yourself to find the answers.

As it always should be. It's our desire to empower others with control of our lives that makes us more sheep than leaders, more seminar attendees than seminar lecturers, more soldiers than generals.

There is nothing wrong with looking for help from experts in the trenches if you are a learner and a beginner and need guidance, leadership, and management. We all have to start somewhere. What better place than to start at the beginning? At least if you start at the beginning you have an assurance that you won't miss anything.

However, after you have acquired the knowledge you must move onward. You can't stay at this level after you've obtained enough experience from these empowered experts.

These people are really looking for experience when they attend seminars or read books. This fact is based on my own experience with what perks them up in both my lectures and writings: war stories from the front. The successes and mistakes of those already in the trenches fascinate them and help them remember the points being made.

I enjoy talking about my experiences and some of the hidden strategies in them because I've learned from them, too, often at great expense to myself. When people ask me about my experiences I often come up with a different twist on the interpretation of the obvious results. This unique observation of common experiences makes the vicarious reliving that more memorable.

Experience, in any form, is beneficial to you as a developing trader. At the time that you are gaining the experience, you might not know what the benefit will be. But if you encounter enough similar experiences, you will know what is important enough to you that you will repeat situations which create similar experiences. That is a major clue to what you must learn to overcome any blocks in your progress to becoming a successful trader.

RULE 39

Both Long- and Short-Term Trades Start Off as Short-Term Trades, but Winning Trades Are Long Term

When you place a trade, you can turn it into a long-term trade, or you can turn it into a short-term trade by closing it out within a short period of time. Whatever the final duration of the trade, the initial trade must be made with the intent or expectation of it being a short-term trade.

The essential difference between a winning trader and a losing trader is how they classify their initial short-term trades.

At the time you initiate a trade, you don't know if it will turn into a profit or a loss. The lack of strict understanding of what is defined as a profit or a loss, even though the trade is not closed, is important in causing you to trade unsuccessfully. If you have a trade that is not closed you have a tendency to believe that whatever it is, a profit or a loss, it isn't affecting your profitability. Nothing could be further from the truth because this trade has to be closed out eventually. If it is an open trade with a profit, closing it out will make it a realized profit; if it is an open trade with a loss, closing it out will make it a realized loss. Note the action that your closing the trade does to the trade: you make it realizable. Prior to this it was an open trade and you had a tendency to believe that this would not damage your equity.

I found a rule that should help you close your losing trade before you get used to the open trade loss as an acceptable situation. (I seldom use this rule myself nowadays, but if you use this rule you should be able to handle the difficult action of getting rid of your losers.) Here, I enter the factor of time to the open trade. If after a certain number of days, if trading long term, or hours, if trading shorter term, the open trade is not showing a profit, I will close it out. I will close the open trade out based on the passing of time. If it shows a loss, the passage of time will force me to close out the trade. If it shows no gain, the passage of time will also force me to close out the trade. However, if the trade starts to show a profit, and the time has passed, I will leave the trade as an open trade. From here I will make sure my stop loss orders follow the market's movement to protect my profits.

You might question why I would need to enter the factor of the passage of time to evaluate an open trade position. You might be wondering why I might not want to use another factor, such as that of price moving against me, as the factor to use in closing out trades. You're correct in concluding that the movement of price against your open trade position is the ultimate reason why you should get rid of your loser, but the inception of the passage of time forces the decision to get rid of losers that much sooner. (A beginning or unseasoned trader or investor needs to get rid of a losing trade sooner because they have not disciplined themselves to take losses based on price activity. Most such traders cannot get to the point of taking a loss. Looking at the factor of time will help the trader or investor to displace the apprehension of taking a loss to another level: getting rid of positions based on time.)

Often if I used the movement of price against my open trade I would wait longer than the initial passage of time I would have set up for the limit to hold my position. Instead of closing out a scratch or a losing trade after three days I have waited as long as three weeks to three months for price to move against me enough so that I was stopped out of my positions. The waiting for the price to move against me enough so that I was stopped out moved me out of my position sure enough, but it also grated upon my nerves while I was waiting. The grating was enough to throw my balance off in other trading situations.

Then, if I've positively taken myself out of a losing or a scratch trade using the factor of time, I will re-enter my position, from the same side, later. I re-enter from the same side because I've not had other indications that my initial position is incorrect. For example, if I've sold out my long position after several days of inactivity in the market I've got positions in, I will try to re-establish a second long position later.

(In a previous example when I told a client to not get rid of his non-moving currency position, but instead to place stop sell orders beneath his entry points, I was considering several other factors. One of them was the obvious commission cost involved in closing out his non-moving positions. Closing out the currency trades without obvious reason would have been expensive for the client. If one is handling retail clients, the act of getting such clients in and out of markets without justifiable reasons would be regarded as churning. The client was also not a daytrader, so placing a stop sell order fitted his requirements better. If he were a daytrader he would have entered and exited the market more frequently and his commission costs would have been lower to accommodate such increased trading activities.)

Now, how should winning trades and losing trades be treated? Throw in the factor of time again. This is important in allowing the markets to perform their miracles for you.

In addition to following my suggestion that you close out scratch or a losing trade within a fixed length of time you should now look at winners with more leniency. Don't close out the winning trades in a few days or a few hours, but let them remain open trades. You would then allow the market to make money for you. In the cases when after the fixed number of days have elapsed and your winner turns into a loser, then your stop sell order should have been in place to take you out of your bad trade. The stop sell order is the final stop-gap measure to protect your equity. There is really nothing that can be done about such situations where your open trade profits turn back to become scratch positions and eventually to become losers. The only thing I can say about this is that the original position was incorrect; your analysis was incorrect. You might want to re-establish your second position in the same direction, but I would caution against this because the chance your analysis is incorrect is greater than before because of the passage of time: time tells all. If the market was incorrectly analyzed by you to begin with, and the market is behaving exactly the way you haven't planned, the reentering from the same side will merely be a repetition of the conclusions from a bad analysis.

So winning trades, i.e., those that show open-trade profits, are treated by winning traders as long-term trades. Losing trades, i.e., those that show open-trade losses, are treated by winning traders as short-term trades and are closed out immediately.

The losers, however, have flipped this around. They keep losing trades on the books and close out winning trades as soon as they can. They hang onto their losers and turn them into long-term trades. The trades they close out immediately are those that show profits immediately.

Now that you understand the differences in duration of trades, and how either a winning or a losing trader views them, execute along the same lines as a winner would.

RULE 40

Arbitrage Plays Are Everywhere

There are many ways to make money in the markets but only a few solid ways to make money consistently. I've found myself in several situations where I was able to exploit a market situation that was topical. Once that area exhausted itself I was forced to look elsewhere since the plays would no longer exist. Still, I suggest that you look outside of the conventional plays to make other opportunities happen.

Arbitrage means the process of buying and selling similar stock, currency, or commodity which are priced differently on different markets. For example, IBM stock is traded both in the United States and in London. If the price of IBM is higher in the United States and lower in London, then the process of arbitrage means the person performing the arbitrage buys the stock in London and sells the stock in the United States and captures the difference between the two prices.

The simplistic arbitrage is the one that everyone knows how to do. The more creative arbitrage situations require more understanding of the mechanics of the markets. The creative arbitrages require considerable research and thoroughness in analysis.

The first example that we'll look at involves a pure stock arbitrage play. The second example also involves an arbitrage play; this is an intermarket play. The third example illustrates and broadens your idea of what an arbitrage should be: a conceptual arbitrage. By leading you through the mental process of stock arbitrage to its broader concept, conceptual arbitrage, I hope to teach you a thinking process which will allow you to make money in all types of markets.

Stock Versus Stock (Like Versus Like)

What would you say if I told you of a market play that costs you absolutely no money? No risk. Nothing. What would you say? Too good to be true? Yes, but some of those plays are around. More often than you would ever believe.

I achieved one of my speculative successes in a company on the verge of bankruptcy. I managed to make a very successful play in it, profits from which I later used to play larger market positions elsewhere.

The company was Chrysler Corporation, which was on the verge of bankruptcy in 1980 when Iacocca was brought in from Ford Motors Corporation to run it.

The play involved something as simple as buying the preferred stock, which has equity risk, and shorting the common stock, as insurance against the company going bankrupt.

What may surprise you is that for the last ten or so years Chrysler has not had a preferred stock issue outstanding. The last one issued by the company was in 1978 when it issued a $2.75 cumulative convertible preferred stock, which was callable by 1983 at $25 per share.

Based on information from *Moody's Industrial Manual* (1978), these were the salient details of the issue: On June 20, 1978, 10,000,000 shares were offered by Merrill Lynch White Weld Capital Markets Group, First Boston Corporation and associates. Each unit consisted of $2.75 preferred stock plus one-half warrant on the common stock. Chrysler Corporation $2.75 cumulative preferred with par value of $25. There were 20,000,000 shares authorized but only 10,000,000 outstanding. It had preference rights over the common stock in dividends and assets (a critical component to the arbitrage play). Holders of the preferred were entitled to cumulative cash dividends at the rate of $2.75 per share per year, payable quarterly. In liquidation, holders are entitled to receive $25 per share plus accrued dividends. This was callable on and after July 1, 1983, on at least 30 but not more than 60 days notice at $25 per share plus accrued dividends.

Figure 40.1 shows the price activity of Chrysler common stock from 1974 to 1985. The price range was from a low of $3.125 to a high of about $45 per share. A price chart of the preferred stock is unavailable since no charting service tracked the preferred issues. I was able to obtain the high-low trading ranges from research materials of the preferred stock on a daily basis which validated the arbitrage play.

Once the company's fundamentals turned bad, the play was to buy the Chrysler preferred and short the Chrysler stock. The price of both issues went down to the $3–$4 level. This was true for both stocks! On April 15, 1982, both stocks touched a low of $3 and a fraction. The difference between the two stocks went as low as $0.50, when the common traded at $4.875 and the preferred traded at $5.25.

My strategy rested on the fact that if the Chrysler Company went down the tubes then the common stock would be worthless. At whatever price I shorted the stock

FIGURE 40.1 Chrysler chart

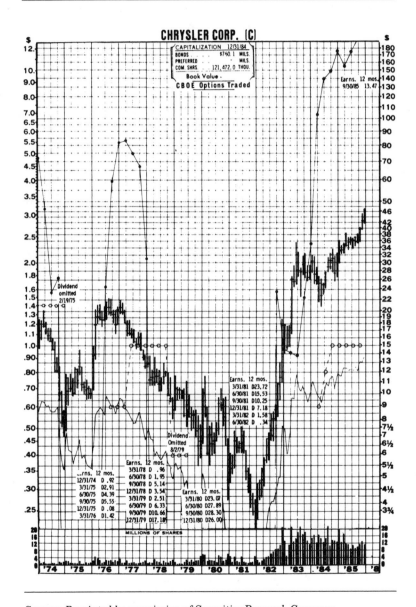

it would eventually go to zero upon bankruptcy liquidation. Meanwhile, the Chrysler preferred I bought would also go down. The difference in what I lost on the preferred versus the money I made on the common stock short would be the actual amount I lost. The spread ranged from $2.00 to $0.50; in a worst-case scenario I would lose no more than $2 per spread play. The upside was limited by the price of the preferred stock. The preferred dividends, even though they weren't paid out because the company had no earnings, accumulated relentlessly.

As the proceedings to get funding for Chrysler's bailout progressed, it appeared as if Chrysler might be able to come back from the grave. The stock market responded. The price of the common rose. The price of the preferred stock rose faster. The widest difference between the two was about $7.50. At that point in the spread, the preferred had risen to the price of about $25 and the common had risen to about $17–$18.

With the spread having widened from a low of $0.50 to $7.50, I figured it was time to take profits. Within less than two years, the return on this arbitrage play was about 500 percent annualized (1½ years holding period, risk of $0.50 to make $7.50). I can't remember what the cumulated dividends on the preferred were, but it came to a positive carry for the spread play! Yikes, they even paid me to hold the positions!

At the point of unwinding the spread, by buying in the short common at $17.50 and selling the preferred at $25, I, the arbitrageur, could have opted to take the $7 net profit and then buy the common stock for an outright hold with the profits. Instead of buying the full amount of shares, the purchase would have been determined by the net profit: for every spread trade profit of one share I could take the $7 net profit and buy a proportionate share of common.

Here is free money in a free position. Watching the common stock rise from this point on is riskless!

Chrysler is now trading at around $60 per share, adjusted for splits. That's another 1000 percent return on the outright position. Once you know how the game on Wall Street is played and how to play it, you can really profit. As a result, the profits from the play further capitalized my trading. Thank you, Chrysler. Thank you, Lee Iacocca.

Stock Versus Similar Value (Like Versus Similar)

The second example of an arbitrage play rests with broadening the concept of arbitraging. To arbitrage stock versus stock isn't necessary!

From a conceptual viewpoint, you can arbitrage anything against anything else; the more obviously removed each of these two arbitragable items are from each other, the greater the potential for profit.

The problem rests with attempting to "create a connection" between two presumed arbitrageable items when realistically there aren't any connections. This is one of the reasons why traders are always looking for correlations between items. The first sign of statistically significant correlations—either positively or negatively correlated—indicates a possible connection. There may not be, in fact, any relevance between the arbitrageable items, but traders must heed this first sign. This germinating point is where potentially lucrative trading situations spring forth. Those who can perceive, not see, the correlations can then trade one item against the other before the rest of the trading community gets hold of these ideas.

A Legal, Profitable Arbitrage Example from an Illegal Action

Eastman Kodak developed a line of instant photography cameras years ago by infringing on the patent

rights of Polaroid Corporation. For several years, Eastman Kodak manufactured their own cameras and sold
their own instant film. One day Polaroid hauled Eastman Kodak into court for violations of Polaroid's instant
camera patents. The case dragged on for years and eventually Eastman Kodak lost one of the largest patent
infringement lawsuits ever filed. Kodak was ordered to
pay $909,000,000 to Polaroid for infringement of five of
the latter's patents.

As this was going on a unique arbitrage play was
occurring.

The settlement involved reimbursing the owners of
instant cameras since Kodak was now no longer able to
manufacture the film. The initial reimbursement package came in the form of coupons for processing film,
credit toward the purchase of other Kodak cameras and
supplies, or a share of stock in Eastman Kodak. As a
stock trader I wasn't interested in the film or cameras,
but I was interested in the stock.

I didn't own an instant camera but I sensed an arbitrage play here: The announcements came across the
broad tape practically every day after Kodak lost the
suit in court. So I monitored the outcome.

I did my research on the camera and found Kodak
sold a lot of them, but I reasoned that not too many people who bought Kodak cameras were that market savvy.
I called up a local discount retail company, McDade
(which has since gone bankrupt), and inquired about the
instant camera. The inventory manager told me they
had 37 new cameras, but had no film for them because
they could no longer be manufactured by Kodak. He told
me that he would sell them to me at $18 a piece. I'm
sure I could have negotiated and taken down the price
to about $10 a piece. Why not? Cameras not being made
anymore and film production ended. What is a holder of
the camera to do? Make his own film so that he can use
the camera?

The price of Eastman Kodak stock was trading at a bit above $50 a share. An arbitrage situation of about $32 a share. Not a bad play.

I immediately scoured around the Chicagoland area for more cameras. I wanted to accumulate 100 cameras and convert to 100 shares of stock. The company was giving me $32 a share to take the cameras back to them. Sounded good to me. While doing this halfheartedly I found 76 more cameras available in the Chicagoland area.

Kodak had set up a toll-free line for dealing with inquiries concerning this reimbursement package. I knew where to get my inventory. I called the toll-free line and inquired how many cameras I could bring in. The operator looked in her instruction manual and could find no mention of how many cameras could be brought in by one person or family. They absolutely had no policy in this matter. I started to think of thousands of cameras. If someone paid me $32 for each camera I could locate and return, I'll stand on my head and do it all day. The beauty of what I was doing was that I could do it in batches. One phone call got me an average of 15 cameras, or a quick $480 for ten minutes or less.

And there was no downside risk. I said to the operator I would call back in a month to get updated information.

Then as I was plotting to pick up the cameras, an announcement came across the tape that a camera owner had sued Eastman Kodak for not offering an additional option: repayment in cash. Now why take the darn thing in cash? The stock is just as good as cash and we were still at the beginning stages of a bull market. The stock would appreciate to $70 in no time flat.

Then began a protracted series of legal proceedings. I'm a stock trader and I wanted the stock. Since there were legal problems with this swap I delayed my acquisition of the Kodak cameras.

As I continued to follow the proceedings I happened to be browsing in a used clothing store with a friend who collects antique jewelry. He knew what he was looking for and every so often he would find a bargain amidst all the junk jewelry. Then an intriguing opportunity presented itself.

While in the store I happened to find a used Kodak instant film camera. I bought it for $5 and promptly sent it in to Kodak for reimbursement, whenever that would occur.

By this time Kodak had implemented a policy to limit the number of instant cameras that one person or family could return. Imagine my chagrin when I found out that I could return no more than ten cameras! Not worth the time of day for me to play around with this anymore!

I received one of about 3,400,000 checks that Kodak sent out that year. The total cost to Kodak on this portion of the settlement came to about $200,000,000 for all the Kodak instant cameras that were sold and returned to Kodak from 1976 to 1986.

The Eastman Kodak/Polaroid situation was minute, but it thoroughly illustrates an arbitrage play that could have made you money on a small scale.

An additional fallout from Eastman Kodak losing on the patent infringement was that Polaroid eventually raised prices on its own line of products because Kodak was no longer making a competing product. So Polaroid really won twice, once in court and once in the stores.

Idea Versus Idea (Conceptual Arbitrage) or: How to Sell a Newsletter Many Times

I've shown you a conventional arbitrage in the strictest sense of the term—stock versus stock—and one involving stock and non-stock. Now let's look at an arbitrage that's conceptual in nature but which you should be able to extrapolate further into the real world.

I was a regular panelist on one of the local television stations for a brokerage company that sponsored a weekly interview show. Three panelists asked questions of an invited industry expert for each taping. The brokerage company taped guests in batches, often interviewing three guests per taping session.

I arrived several minutes early for the taping of this show and sat in the waiting room. One of the other guests, Dennis Dunn of the money management firm Dunn & Hargitt, had arrived earlier from Indiana. Prior to getting into the money management area they had been publishers of point and figure charts. I knew the reputation of Dunn & Hargitt so I was a bit awed to be in the same sitting room with this man who was a partner in the firm.

As we were waiting for our taping we engaged in conversation. I always like to find out what people's background are, to understand where they are coming from. Dennis Dunn was a pleasant person, nonobtrusive and very congenial. He was classy.

The conversation delved into the early beginnings of the Dunn & Hargitt Company. Dunn told me they hadn't always been involved in the markets. They were first a publisher of a monthly newsletter on child development. Their company published a monthly newsletter which was sent out every month to subscribers who were raising children.

I asked Dunn how they got the names to solicit directly. He told me they would find lists of newborns from hospitals and solicit their families in a direct mail piece on the benefits of subscribing to their child development newsletter.

I commented that writing a newsletter was very tough work. I mumbled to Dennis Dunn that he had to block out two weeks for each issue, so I sympathized with him on the amount of work that had to go into each and every issue of the newsletter.

Dunn replied that he had no more work to do. At this point he said all he had to do was this: market the newsletter, fill the subscription order, and bill the subscribers. I was puzzled. I asked him whether or not he hired people to write the newsletter, and he said no and that he and his earlier associates were the ones who wrote the newsletters. I was even more puzzled. Then he proceeded to explain to me what he had done so he now no longer needed to write the newsletter.

Here was a newsletter publisher who never had to write a newsletter any more! Another conundrum in life!

In the early development of the newsletter he and his partners had created each issue from scratch. This was the hardest part. Each issue detailed to the parents what they could expect from their developing babies. One month separated the issues. So, the first issue was for a one-month old baby; the second month's issue was for a two-month old baby, and so forth.

Once their company had created this inventory of newsletters, they had everything they needed. This set of newsletters then had to be marketed. The products were there! All they needed to do was to find a newborn to a new set of parents and essentially sell them the newsletter "series." When a baby was one-month old Dunn pulled out the master for the one-month newsletter and sent it. When the baby was two months old, Dunn pulled out the second newsletter, made a copy of it, and sent it out. This went on until the child became an adolescent. (For a detailed write-up about this see "Starting Your Own Newsletter" by Berkeley Rice, *Money* magazine, March 1984.)

Where was the arbitrage situation here, you might ask? It's a bit more difficult to perceive in this example because it is more subtle, but it is distinctly an arbitrage. But this example will allow you to make yourself a millionaire, if you can find a similar arbitrage situation.

This is how the arbitrage situation worked. There are two entities: the newsletter series and the new baby. The newsletter series had been created earlier and all the knowledge on the development of a baby was encompassed in its pages. To the baby, everything at the time of birth was completely new—"new" desires, needs, demands, etc. But what is new to the baby and the parents isn't really new. From the perspective of the information contained in the newsletter, nothing was new; in fact, it could be considered old information, but it's new to each new mom and dad.

Dunn had managed to "leg" into a time-based spread which is another way to look at an arbitrage situation. The elegance of this situation entailed no open market risk! He was long the "infinite time" side and picked and chose his time sensitive side to offset against. The infinite time side was the set of newsletters; this product seldom, if ever, aged. The physical, mental, and emotional development of the child were encompassed within the pages of the newsletter. The children to fit into this developmental mode were constantly being born, always going through these stages of development, which were naturally found in the newsletters. This was brilliant!

At any moment in time, the newborn, had he or she known it, could have asked Dunn for copies of the newsletter from future editions or even from past editions. At the age of six the newborn could have read what he was to be like at the age of 15! At any moment in time, the newborn had access to information from the past and the future! But because the newborn was not aware of this, and most likely neither were the parents, no such foreknowledge was available.

From other people's broader experiences, the concept of knowing the future is possible and highly probable because the past, present and future exist now! This example is simplistic, but the concept is the same: this is

239

an example of forecasting. The markets have already been etched out in stone. To be able to accurately "forecast" them, like the newsletter writer who found the right newsletter to send at the right time in the baby's life, we merely have to find the right model to base our forecasts.

How can you extend this conceptual arbitrage into your real life? Start by looking for situations which are similar to the Eastman Kodak/Polaroid situation. Once you see how this works, then you can move the concept of arbitrage completely out of the stock realm and into real life which this child development newsletter pointed out.

RULE 41

We All Make Mistakes, but We Mustn't Allow Our Emotions To Obstruct Our Learning Process

You confront many situations in the trading arena in which you most likely make the wrong choices and lose money. In retrospect, there is only one straight and narrow path for making money in the markets. On that path you'll be traversing a lot of other paths which will cause you to make mistakes. Most of these sidepaths are not financial disasters, but any one of them can be if you allow them.

For example, a sidepath which might distract you from trading successfully could be as simple as your being fixated on some specific trading strategy. I know some people who have hooked onto using Japanese Candlestick charting and have made it their mission to study every aspect of it. Candlestick charting is a set of specific daily price patterns which forecast future price movements. Others have fixated on using moving averages and have become experts at every nuance of these momentum indicators. Once these techniques start to overwhelm you to the exclusion of anything else, then you've allowed these to become more important than the real reason to trade or invest in the markets: make money.

Similar to Hindu philosophy, in the trading world you will continue to make the same mistakes over and over again until you get it right. Then you must remove the mistakes from obstructing your success. You can become successful only by undergoing this initial trial and error period and then making a conscious effort to remove your obstructions.

Each of us has our own set of backgrounds. We grew up in different environments. In the process of using the support systems our parents have given to us, we are able to achieve our objectives. I'm not discussing the fact that some of us may not know what our objectives are. The floundering that most of us have done in our youth was merely attempts at finding goals and objectives worth achieving. These attempts aren't necessarily failures but a way to eliminate less necessary goals and objectives.

Depending on our emotional and psychological makeup what we would consider to be less than desirable as a goal would be highly treasured by others. This isn't even an issue of right or wrong. It's an issue of discovering what is out there that can provide enough motivation for you to seek it out and perfect it.

A danger rests in the following scenario, however. In the process of eliminating less than desirable goals we go through the process of working with those goals, striving for them, and when the objectives are within reach achieving them doesn't always satisfy us as we expected. Was pursuing them a mistake? Of course not. They're part of our own search for our own truths, our own personal objectives.

In trading the markets there are many actions you can create to make yourself more successful, i.e., make money in the markets. There are many different ways to tackle that objective. Some of us initially, because of our inexperience in the trading business, get sidetracked on the way to achieving the ultimate goal by the excitement and thrills of the chase. The game itself becomes the goal.

Choosing the game itself as the goal is neither right nor wrong if that's what you're really after. Many times I've confronted unsuccessful traders, those who weren't able to make money. I asked them what they would like to do rather than battle it out every day in the pits or from the upstairs trading room. Few are honest enough, or even conscious enough of their actions, to say that they would rather be doing something else. The few who do recognize and can verbalize it eventually wind up doing something else. This is their continued search to satisfy their needs.

Like any profession, successful trading isn't always thrilling. It entails a large degree of boredom. The exhilaration and excitement of risk-prone trading that we are led to believe to be "correct" trading is only the peripheral elements of trading. Yes, you can let these two elements of trading be the driving force to your trading. Unless you address the point that trading is often humdrum, then you will never be able to make money in the markets.

Mistakes, therefore, are the results of unsatisfactory searches for satisfying your goals and objectives. That's all they are.

It's only when you attach feelings of rejection to mistakes that there are problems in your search for goals. You mustn't do this.

If you attach personal rejection to your mistakes you condition yourself to eliminate undesirable goals less efficiently. Why is this so? When you personalize market rejection into a rejection of you as a person you will build up defense mechanisms which will shield you from

243

personal sensitivities. This will prevent you from looking at problems objectively in the future. Frankly, it
hurts to be rejected personally. In the process of building
up the defense mechanisms you create extended
responses. So instead of taking loss in your position
because it went against you, you're saying to yourself
that the position should be held because the market
reports were wrong. Once you deceive yourself into per-
ceiving the market reports weren't aligning to your position it's not that difficult for you to think other factors
beyond your obvious control influenced those developments. When does it stop? When should it stop? Certainly not further away from the source of your problem:
your losing position. The best way to deal with your losing position is to get rid of it as soon as possible. Otherwise, the chain from action to reaction becomes more
complex and distracting. Eventually it will even
lengthen more. You will have allowed the problem and
the solution to the problem to be separated from each
other. As a result, future attempts at resolving the ger-
minated problem really become difficult!

RULE 42

Those Who Lose Money Lose Much, Those Who Lose a Friend Lose More, but Those Who Keep Their Spirit Keep All

Losses, losses, losses. By the way we behave in our everyday lives you would think that preventing losses is our primary reason for existence, wouldn't you? My secret philosophy is that since I came into this world without anything, when it comes time to leave this existence, everything I have accumulated . . . well it's going to be lost. Can't figure out a way to prevent this from happening . . . yet.

Money: I've made a lot of it and lost a lot of it, too. **The winning trades bothered me at first: couldn't wait to take the profits**. After I rectified my thinking so that I could actually feel good about winners I concentrated on increasing my trading size so that I could make more absolute dollar amounts on each trade.

Along with the increased trading size, my losses, when I was wrong, got bigger and bigger. (The positive offset to this was that the amount of trading capital got larger and larger, and the losses as a percentage of trading capital, got smaller and smaller!) The bad feelings about losses also mounted, especially when they were apt to get larger and larger. So I retrained my thinking to live with the losses and learned from them; I desensitized myself to the losses. When I started to get into five-figure losses in wrong trading plays, it was at first traumatic. Having the ability to lose in one play what the average person makes in one year in income bewildered me. But as time wore on I became less sensitive to this and learned to live with it.

Once I got to the point of losing six figures on several plays, the losses didn't bother me any more. Oh sure, it bothered me that I was stupid enough to have gone for those dumb plays. Getting suckered on bad plays was more aggravating than just losing the money.

Let me tell you a little observation: Money isn't always what it's cracked up to be. It is, however, the most expeditious way to convert a majority of your goals to reality, so keep your wins and losses in perspective.

What truly is important, however, is people and your relationships with them. By cultivating your relationships with others, you can make lasting changes and have impact. Your life has meaning.

I have a good friend I've known for over 15 years. He and I started trading together at the Chicago Board of Trade in the Treasury bond pit in the late '70s.

Over the years he developed his own methods of scalping and spreading between the Treasury bonds and Treasury notes. Once he found his little niche he consistently made $250,000 a year.

Several years ago, he told me that he hadn't been making the money that he once had. After years of making money he had started losing money or not making it consistently. Then he showed me his last trading statement.

What had caused this? In mid-1992, he went to the floor to trade the Treasury bonds. As he was putting on positions, a runner ran into the pit and knocked my friend out of the pit. My friend tumbled out of the pit and landed on his head, receiving a concussion and injuring his spinal column.

Because of this accident, the last several years have been very difficult for him. He is now no longer able to do simple mathematical calculations in his head; he has a hard time fixating on simple math problems.

He oscillated between periods of elation and depressions. But he didn't allow his injuries to stop him. Watching my friend cope taught me people make and move the world, not ideas nor money. As long as he had spirit, he could make a comeback. Spirit, hope, or wish, whatever you call it, is the optimism in life which will help you overcome the difficulties.

So after he showed me his trading statement, as a friend I began tracking and monitoring his results. He recently embarked on a path to get back into the business in another form. Despite this debilitating accident he had the spirit to come back. With therapy and support from family members he took the alternative track: managing money.

For the last year and a half he has laid the groundwork to trade in an environment which is less dependent upon his former natural skill and talent, rapid math calculations. He created a commodity trading pool, hired a computer programmer to implement his trading ideas and raised over $500,000 for management. He is well on his way to becoming successful again.

My friend has found another avenue to success in the trading world. If you have the drive to succeed, you, too, will succeed wherever you are and at whatever you are doing. My friend has the spirit to keep going despite what most would consider to be a formidable task: getting his financial life in order once some of his former abilities have been laid to waste.

So, when you encounter difficulties in trading, know that the problems you face are only insurmountable from your immediate perspective. Others have confronted similar ones. Some allowed the problems to waste them; others took the opposite tack by facing the problems directly and overcoming them.

You are your own profit center. No one and nothing else can make the profits for you, but with the right spirit no one and nothing else can keep you from making those profits, except you.

RULE 43

To Come Out Ahead, Do Not Keep Repeating Your Mistakes

If you want to come out ahead, do not keep repeating your mistakes. In this way you will eventually succeed. Remember, also, that the market always gives you a thousand and one opportunities for new errors. So be on guard!

I am a successful professional trader for two very good reasons.

First, I know my business. I know things the public investor and trader are not aware of. I know how to get good fills and good executions. I know what to look for in a sales pitch by a broker. I know all the things over 20 years of experience have given me. Yet this knowledge isn't the sole reason for my success.

There were times when I forgot to exercise some call options. At other times I forgot to buy my calls back to prevent the owners from exercising them. Once I took delivery of thousands of bushels of corn and didn't know they were sitting somewhere in the granaries with my name tagged on them. Or, what about the time I went in buying beans when I should have been buying bonds. I also vividly recall the time I spent ten minutes on the phone arguing with the phone clerk who couldn't execute my wheat orders. As I found out later, he was running for the firm I had specifically set up for trading the NYFE Index. One of many, many mistakes.

I made these mistakes when I didn't have the experience, but I corrected them and then found better solutions to the problems. As a phone clerk 23 years ago I executed buy and sell orders in stocks for our firm traders. Several wirehouses were sending orders to us for execution. Depending on how much business their firm gave us in commodities we rationed our stock orders to them. One wirehouse one day, another one the next.

One day I inadvertently entered a buy order instead of a sell order. The firm trader was doubled up on his position. This error went into an errors and omissions account.

I corrected that problem by using two wirehouses every day afterwards. Before the market opened I specifically told one wirehouse they were going to get all the buy orders for that day and told the other wirehouse that they would get sell orders. This prevented me from entering the wrong side orders. If I tried to enter a buy order to a sell-side wirehouse the wirehouse's clerk would correct me before the trades were transacted. Today some of the brokerage companies have implemented this self-correcting method. The frequency of my wrong-side orders subsequently dropped to zero because I saw the problem and rectified it by implementing self-corrective procedures.

As I progressed in my field I made fewer mistakes and became more professional.

This is exactly what you must do to become a professional trader who makes money consistently and frequently. You cannot allow the ease of entering this business to deceive you into believing that laxity in this business is similar to laxity in any other business. You must not believe mistakes in this business are easily forgiven. This business is not similar to other businesses and the mistakes are not forgivable. I have been called a hard person to work with, but I know my business and know my parameters. I'm an easygoing person on the surface, but when it comes to trading and all peripheral strategies I am a professional.

The second main reason for my professional success is that I don't like to make mistakes. Mistakes reflect stupidity and poor planning. It looks bad, it's sloppy, and it smacks of negligence.

However, if you are a relatively new trader, you can let yourself make some mistakes, and build them into your career. Say to yourself you will allow yourself to make, for example, one stupid mistake in a two-day period. If you don't make one mistake in that two-day period, you're closer to becoming a professional. If you make more than what you've allotted, you have to learn from the mistakes. If you continue to make more mistakes than you've allowed yourself, then you must raise your number of mistakes acceptable to you. If you continue doing this, get out of the business. You're not cut out for it.

To be a professional trader, you must find ways to eliminate or modify the environment that causes mistakes.

We will make errors in analysis as long as we are alive, plus the trading business is a chance business to begin with. We cannot be totally sure until later that our current decisions and actions will be appropriate.

To reduce the risk of mistakes, I also limit the amount of capital I place on each trade. On the improbable chance that I may be absolutely wrong, I don't want to be absolutely taken out of the trading business.

My most expensive mistakes have shown me that it is never appropriate to go bust.

I'm a professional trader because I make fewer mistakes than the average investor. And when I make those mistakes, I've already made sure they don't nail me to the wall. I've got a backup. Right behind that I have a redundant backup.

These are my own little mental games I've developed to insure that I succeed in trading. For example, I will determine that I want to go long in the Treasury bonds. My first backup is that I use stop sell orders to protect my bond positions once I enter them. Before I enter a long position in bonds I will look to short something else that's weak, perhaps gold. This is my redundant backup. I'm long bonds and short gold, both positions protected by stop orders.

RULE 44

Trade Evenly
and Consistently

$\mathbf{T}$rade evenly and consistently. Do not buy 100 shares today and 1,000 shares tomorrow. Make the distinction between trading size and investing with capital.

Imagine that you are a contractor building a house. You work from the blueprints, the proportions of which correspond to the measurements of the actual building materials.

After the house is built you discover that the one and only yardstick available to you to measure all your materials was not 36 inches but 35 inches in length. All your measurements are off by one inch.

Yet, your house is still standing. Everything is off one inch or a defined proportion of one inch. Do you tear down the house and rebuild? Of course not. You just give everything a fixed one-inch "accommodation" factor. For example, new siding you install later might have half an inch cut from the left side and half an inch cut from the right side. You make up for the known discrepancy, the one inch that's literally built into the house.

Let's take another situation. Your mother-in-law decides to build a similar house adjoining your lot. You conjure up a "magical" yardstick that varies in length from 35 to 37 inches, depending on the user's mood. The angrier the person who is using it, the longer it extends out to 37 inches. The happier and sweeter soul measures with a 35-inch yardstick.

You, the beloved in-law, have three approaches: you can make your mother-in-law mad all the time; you can make her happy and sweet all the time; or you can vary your treatment of her. Her mood and therefore her house ultimately depend on your whim.

In the first two situations, she will be measuring all materials consistently either at 37 inches all the time or at 35 inches all the time. In either case, the house constructed will be off by one inch, which can be accommodated in future development.

But heaven help your mother-in-law if the yardstick varies from 37 to 35 inches. Not only will she be completely frustrated she will never be able to start the construction, let alone finish it.

What do these examples of building a house with a varying yardstick have to do with trading?

Often most of those who are unsuccessful at trading don't consider the basics when initiating trades. But remembering the basics is so critical for future results. This example of building a house with a consistent yardstick illustrates that you mustn't ignore something as simple as varying the size of your trades.

Do not buy more than usual unless you decide your scope of trading in advance. Your percentage of winners to losers will not work out if you vary the amounts continually. For example: If out of ten trades of a 100 shares each you sustain a loss on a final eleventh trade of 1,000 shares, your net profits will be gone! However, if you continue trading in 100 share lots and you have a loss, you will have ten winners and only one loser and still have a net profit. Always be in balance.

I'm always fond of systematic trading approaches. I've learned the hard way that you must always be systematic. One of the ramifications of not being systematic is that you will treat the market in an erratic fashion. Your own erratic trading and the market's own inherent erratic nature will cause large losses.

For example, several years ago I attended a conference on trading techniques. The speaker that evening was discussing her favorite timing technique. Sitting next to me at the back of the lecture hall was an elderly woman who traded the markets from a non-professional perspective.

During the coffee break I discussed techniques and strategies with this attendee. When we came upon an apparently interesting subject—wins and losses using a specific technique—the woman became much more animated.

She told me she had a technique that made money all the time. Wonderment filled my head. I then asked detailed questions such as:

1. *What is defined as making money all the time?* Did it mean that every trade was a profit? Or, did she mean that all trades, as a group, made money in a particular accounting period, such as weekly, monthly, or yearly? She was sketchy here. She didn't recall.
2. *What was defined as a profit?* Was a one-tick profit considered a profit? Or, were profits based on closed trades, regardless of how long it took to close them? She was vague here also. She didn't know.
3. *What was defined as losses?* She hesitated here since she couldn't really pin down the definition. I

considered it crucial since losses will debilitate traders. How she defined losses was variable, also. Sometimes she would put on a trade and keep it open till the losses were several points. At other times, she would arbitrarily close them out. She had no systematic way of defining losses.

4. *What was her trading size?* Here again she couldn't identify them. Sometimes she traded 100 shares of stock; at other times she traded 500 shares. She used only one qualifying rule: she would buy more of something if it were cheaper in price and she bought less of something if it were higher priced. This is fine to use, too, but she would also buy a lot of a higher-priced stock if she had a good "feeling" about it; this negated any "systematic" approach she thought she had developed.

I walked away from the conversation with this woman realizing that a majority of traders and investors get into the markets with a generalized concept of what they want to accomplish.

These people get into the markets without a predefined idea of what are acceptable losses and profits for them. They also get into the markets with no knowledge of what commitment size they have to the markets. They also confuse commitment size per trade with commitment of capital per trade.

Unfortunately, these commitments are first defined for them by their brokers, who ask the first of many questions: How much money do you have to trade with?

This is fine, and required, but these brokers don't follow up that initial question with the further questions and application of sound trading approaches: since you have so much money, we should portion out 10 percent of that capital to this investment or speculation and then a second 10 percent to this, etc. Instead the brokers merely suggest that for that amount of money they have a hot play for a $10 stock. If the price of the hot play was priced at $20, the brokers would buy half as much.

So whether you are measuring to build your house or your investments, use a consistent yardstick.

RULE 45

Intermediate Movements of Stock Prices Can Be Discerned Profitably

When the ticker tape has been going in a certain direction, either up or down, and it comes to a stop for a few seconds, that usually signifies a new chapter is starting. Sometimes it may be a stronger continuation in the same direction. More often, however, it indicates the market may soon turn in the opposite direction.

When I started in the trading business for a third market house (a type of market, not the number of houses I traded for) in 1971, we still had the ticker tape that chattered incessantly during market hours. In our age of electronics, all I see are flashing numbers on a computer screen. The pre-computer era tape broadcasted the vital trade information: name of stock or commodity, price at which the trade occurred, and the number of shares traded of the stock (no volume figures were displayed for commodity transactions).

As the tape chattered, droning onward, my ears picked up on its rhythm. When the markets became active, the chatter picked up and you could hear the paper tape stream faster. When the markets slowed down the tape slowed to a crawl.

A professional ticker tape reader could literally "read" the supply and demand going into and out of stocks. The tape reader could then gauge prospective rallies and selloffs. This was from the intuitive side.

On the logical side, the observation of the type and size of transaction and length of time that separated trades gave further clues and indications of support and resistance.

It was a game played among equals throughout the world where the ticker tape information was broadcasted.

When prices ran up and then paused, you could sense an increase in the supply of stocks or commodities to keep the price increase down or even reverse the price temporarily. You had more assurance that price increases would be kept down and less assurance that prices would reverse by going up. However, when they did reverse, they went down to unforecastable levels, unforecastable with the mere information of watching price movements up and down. The more capable tape readers would know from what congestion or price staging areas prices could fall back to. They were always aware of these price markers and paid particular attention to price action if and when prices got back to these levels. These were the professional tape readers' sign posts on the speculative highways.

Nowadays the advance in technology has created a whole new breed of traders whose only sign posts are relationships. Since there are no longer any physical manifestations of market activities through the chatter of the ticker tape these new traders must find and use whatever information they have available. What they have, and have a lot of, are prices of transactions.

Making do with what they have, instead of ticker tape trading, they electronically trade by quickly calculating relationships between markets. They base their trading decisions on relative price movements between the two markets. The better mental wizards will study price relationships among many different markets and immediately find price discrepancies, i.e., spread price shifts, and jump on them for minuscule profits. Even in this rarefied atmosphere dependent on innate mathematical talents the onset of technology has diminished this edge. Powerful personal computers can do dronelike relationship calculations faster than any human mind can. Having powerful computers puts me on par with even the fastest mathematical idiot savant.

Without current tools of market analysis, it is more difficult to assess market supports or resistances from mere price movement hesitations. This doesn't mean that support or resistance levels aren't existent; discovering them now requires different tools. From the conventional perspective of watching price action we find that prices can go through supports or resistances and then come right back. Price no longer holds for supports or resistance. From the tools that have been developed recently, however, price cannot go through areas of large volume activities. The emphasis on volume is the key to correctly being able to read support and resistance activities in our current trading environment.

RULE 46

Trade Countertrend with a Portion of Your Original Commitment

According to an old trading rule, "When the market is in an up-trend and you wish to take advantage of a little shake-out to come, trade short, but only with ⅓ of the capital used on the long-side. If you usually purchase 300 shares on the up-side, trade only 100 shares short. The reverse is true of a downtrend market.'

I had not read anything that showed specifically how to vary your position risk to minimize equity loss in case your analysis is incorrect. Then I read this rule.

This rule specifically tells you how much you should risk on countertrend trades. Most of us have always presumed that we risk a portion of our total position commitment, not of our total equity, on trending trades, but we were never sure, or at least never aware, of how much to risk of our total commitment, if any, in countertrend trades. We presumed that if we traded 300 shares from the long side in bullish markets, we would also risk 300 shares in countertrend trades.

I had always dismissed trading against the trend anyway, so to take ½, ⅓, or any fraction of the amount I would normally risk on trend trades and put it up against the risks in countertrend trades had not occurred to me. I learned from the market's brute force that it didn't make sense for me to trade against the trend. I'm not that lucky that I can skirt damage by trading against the major market trend. At most, I would just sell out previously established longs at over-bought conditions in bull markets.

In the past, when I needed some action, an "action-fix" so to speak, and the markets were in a corrective phase, I would take a flyer on a few lots of futures or shares of stock. In the back of my mind I was always mindful to get out of those trades speedily if the market resumed its primary trend. Generally, taking flyers didn't make or lose a lot of money for me. Taking flyers merely served to appease my yet untempered need for action.

Let's use an example to see the problem with the rule in this chapter: The market is in a sustained bull move to the upside; any day now it's headed for a correction. You have established long positions of 9,000 shares of stock, or commodities, which you've picked up at cheaper prices. You have large unrealized capital gains. What do you do in this scenario?

Close to a presumed intermediate top you can perform any of the following three actions with your positions and take the results:

1. You can sell out all your longs, stay out of the market completely and look for other trade opportunities. The majority of new to intermediate traders do exactly this and wind up kicking themselves for missing a big portion of a bull market move.

2. You can sell out none of your longs and stay in the markets. Here you are really a long-term trader

and will hold to your long positions come hell or high water. This type of investor makes money, but not as much as a trader-type who can deftly move correctly in and out of the markets to take advantage of the market's intermediate savings.

3. You can sell out part of your longs and stay out of the market until you see a better price opportunity to get back in.

The benefits of choosing one of these three options depend on which method will make you the most money. It's not a question of not ringing the cash register. You already have profitable positions so it's merely a decision of taking them or not, and if taken, how much of the profits to realize.

The next set of options centers on what type of risk you should now take. Remember that if you choose one of these next four options, treat it as a separate trade from whatever choice you made on the first set of three options.

Then you attempt to take advantage of a correction that's due to come by choosing one of the following four:

1. You can sell short 9,000 shares of stock after you've unloaded your longs in the above manner.
2. You can sell short ⅓ of your long commitment, i.e., 3,000 shares after you've unloaded your longs in the above manner.
3. You can stay out of the market by not going short any commitment after you've unloaded your longs in the above manner.
4. You can sell more than your initial position of 9,000 shares, perhaps 12,000 shares, to take advantage of the ensuing correction.

From my own trading experience I would not sell short 9,000 or more shares of stock. I would elect not to

263

short, and I would also stay out of the market on the correction. I would sell short a partial commitment if I wanted a little market action, however.

I base my decisions on several reasons. First, the market has not shown me that the main uptrend has reversed. Markets do not usually stop abruptly and head in the opposite direction overnight. Unfortunately, most of us recall the few exceptions when the market has done this. However, markets need time to reverse directions. So until a bit of time has passed I would continue to buy the market. Until this happens I refrain from shorting.

Second, if I were forced to try to go short I would not take on more positions than originally intended. If I had ridden the move to the upside with 9,000 shares, my profits on the 9,000 shares is there. Let's now figure out what happens when I decide to trade a larger number of shares at the supposed top of the market. I would now expose myself to an additional risk that I did not burden myself with on the way up. With a position of 9,000 shares, a $2.00 move up makes an $18,000 profit. With a position of 12,000 shares, to lose that $18,000 profit all the stock has do is to move against me by $1.50. The chance of a stock, regardless of market position, moving $1.50 in either direction in a day to day fluctuation is better than it moving $2.00.

Why put myself in a greater risk position for losses than the risk position to make the profits? Unfortunately, a majority of investor or traders do this. They trade a constant number of shares on the way to profits and then somewhere at the top they double up the number of shares traded, not necessarily going in the opposite direction of the previous trend, and get taken out of all profits with a normal market reversal. The markets have behaved as always; so have the unsuccessful traders who at the market tops placed all their accumulated profits at risk by increasing their position risk.

Now comes manipulating the market by shorting a number of shares smaller than the original commitment to make the profits. If you wanted to take advantage of the market's supposed down move, shorting a small position is better than shorting a large position. Still, shorting no position, while the market is still bullish, is better than shorting anything.

I can offer an alternative to the above four choices that has worked out well for me: While the markets are still bullish, instead of shorting the very stock that I am making bullish plays in, I would short another stock which is technically weaker. I would then be long a strong stock and short a weak stock, a spread between stocks of different strengths in a bull market.

Here again, depending on market stages and conditions, the stock I short in a still generally bullish market will often turn out to go neither up nor down. It acts as the dead leg of a spread.

Hedge funds essentially operate in this manner, however. This now leads us to the next rule on how you can use the market to absorb huge amounts of capital.

RULE 47

If There Are Large Amounts of Capital, Employ Hedging

All market professionals have an aversion to market risks because these risks are, by definition, uncontrollable.

As professionals, traders have honed certain strategies or methodologies related to their special niche of moneymaking. For example, the scalper goes in and makes a trade by selling over the last sale and buying under the last sale. In this manner the scalper makes his tick, day in and day out. The arbitrageur will buy IBM stock traded in London and sell the stock traded in New York for a small price differential. The options market maker will neutralize his or her net delta positions by hedging the other side in the actual cash market.

Professionals are risk averse. Because they thrive in market risk environments they appear to be risk takers. They aren't.

On the contrary they will seek to "pass off" the risk to others as soon as possible. Note how many bookies in

Las Vegas, who are professionals, will ever take on a bet without finding a way to pass off the risk to someone else? Note also, in the corporate world, how insurance companies through the use of the information derived from actuarial tables, seek to limit their risks? If need be they will pass off risks to re-insurance companies if they can't pass off their risks in their normal channel of operations.

The same applies to huge stock traders. Market risks are those unknown, unseen forces which cause the market to drop precipitously or rally like a rocket. Assassinations of political leaders, interest rate hikes, earthquakes, and other natural disasters, are some of the factors which translate into market risks for professionals.

Professionals develop methods and strategies to insulate themselves from these market risks. One strategy is to be perfectly long and short at all times in the stock market. Let's take a look at how this is done and how best to execute this strategy.

If you have $1,000 to trade the markets you really only buy stock. You couldn't short stock without opening a margin account. You might buy 300 shares of Tucson Electric Power, now trading at $3.50 a share. This is all you can do. If the company goes bad, your money is gone. However, the risk is only $1,000. The chances of a company which came out of reorganization going down is slim, but the stock can easily drop if there's an earthquake in Arizona. Natural disasters can have bearish effects on the most bullish stock. How does one guard against this risk?

For the trader who has large amounts of capital another avenue is open to reduce market risks: hedge trading. Simply, it involves simultaneous entering long and short positions in different stocks. For every long position entered in one stock, a short position must be entered in another stock. In this manner the larger trader is immunized against market risk and concentrates on the individual strengths or weaknesses of the stocks which he positions. (Large commodity trading advisors use futures contracts instead of stocks as their investment vehicles; similarly, bond traders use different maturities of their bonds.)

An assassination of a political leader or an earthquake which destroys a financial center will have no market risk effect on the large trader's net positions. The long positions will drop as much as the short positions. The net effect will be the same. He loses $20 each share on the long stock, but he makes back $20 each share on each short stock. Result: zero loss or profit. Yet, through the correct application of technical decision-making tools, the trader is long the strongest stock and short the weakest stock. He makes money in this manner; but he doesn't lose money to market risk.

Having successfully neutralized market risk as it affects his portfolio the large trader can now put more capital to work. This hedge concept approach is now a monstrous juggernaut which ingests unlimited capital and excretes neatly packaged but matched (in many senses) long/short market risk pairs of stocks.

Because of the large amount of capital they have at their disposal to trade and invest in markets the hedgers' basic strategy mitigates against unforecastable events; one countertrend position acts as an insurance hedge against the possibility that these events can and do occur.

If the large trader has already picked the two stocks he wants to be both long and short, he must put those two trades on. How does he go about doing it? He works the more difficult of the two stocks first. Once he has that side done, then he goes to the other side which is the more liquid. Let's say he has decided to buy IBM stock and short Digital Equipment stock as the paired hedge stock. IBM is considerably more liquid than Digital

Equipment. He executes his position in Digital Equipment first, and then goes to execute his IBM side. When it comes time to unwind the position, he repeats the same strategy: execute the less liquid stock first, then close the transaction by doing the more liquid side.

The strategy is not as simplistic as this chapter implies because, like anything else in life, the actual application of any concept always brings unforeseen problems. Other nuances and eye-opening problems can occur when you implement these strategies to take advantage of huge amounts of capital. This chapter has explained only the core concept of reducing market risk.

RULE 48

Stop Loss Orders Are Most Effective at Certain Stages of Market Action

According to a trading psychology book from the early 1900s, "Stop loss orders are most effective in the late stage of a Bull market. That is just the time to use extreme caution. In the early stages, however, 'stop-losses' may sever you from the limb of the tree which you may be sitting on. The object of stops is to prevent losses and long tie-ups of capital."

The issue of whether or not to use stop loss orders has always been hotly debated. In my own case I've always used stop loss orders "to prevent losses and long tie-ups of capital." At times I might have been lax by not entering a stop loss order to protect my open position, but most of the time within three days of the execution of the entry order I've always had stop loss orders in place.

However according to the above rule note the market condition under which stop loss orders should not be used. The rule advises not to use stop loss orders in the early stages of a bull market because they assume that your position will be stopped out with losses while the market is building for a runaway stage later.

Yes, and no is all I can say to this contention. I've always used stop lost orders in trading ranges which eventually turned out to be bases upon which massive bull markets spring forth. I've also used them in trending markets. I do not discriminate among the types of markets I trade: the stop loss orders are there always!

The positioning of my stop orders in trading range, base-building markets have always been far enough away from the general range of the market that these stop loss orders seldom got caught. If and when they do get caught I always re-enter the market, so this precludes losing out on a bullish position in a base-building market. I take my wounds, but I also get back in.

This is a perfect example of employing a *set of strategies* that is so in tune with the markets that each strategy by itself points to an overall correct trading strategy: I enter long positions in base-building markets; I enter stop loss orders in case I am wrong; and if I am taken out of my positions, *I re-enter from the long side again.* The first rule by itself implies that the practitioner of the rule doesn't have a general trading strategy; that is, in base-building markets, entering a stop loss order will remove you from a long position before the market charges up. This rule implies that you will not re-enter the market long.

The sensitivity some traders have to the type of markets they're trading, and whether or not they will have an increased or decreased chance of getting their stops caught, explains why these people have told me that they never place stop loss orders in the markets to protect their positions and wind up making huge profits!

Because these traders have always positioned in trading range markets, and not runaway markets, this allowed them the luxury of not using stop loss orders and still never setting themselves up for potentially huge losses. The damage done to one's open positions in trading range markets is minimal, with or without stop loss orders in place; in runaway markets, if and when the markets reverse, the damage to one's equity can be severe if not protected with stop-loss orders.

The two groups of traders—one using stops all the time and the other never using stops—are all basically entering positions at the base-building periods. Stops placed here, if entered at all, and then if caught, will close out their positions at minimal losses, but losses still. **In cases like these, taking the open positions without being stopped out is just as good, if not better than getting caught on the low of the trading range base with stop orders!** Especially if once you get caught on the stop you are inclined to go in the opposite direction, i.e., not continue to be long but to take the short position!

Without knowing it, these investors or traders have predefined their supposed "violation" of the stop loss rule. The conditions under which they don't use stop loss orders have minimized the chances of getting stopped out, and also have created a condition whereby they can get stopped out often on the low of the trading range lows and still climb back on board for a possible sustained move. So they are perfectly right in what they are propounding: no stop loss orders, ever, and it just so happens that these traders always position themselves in base-building markets.

This is part of the work that you as a thinking trader must do. Now that you've figured out that it is okay to never use stops because you only want to position in base-building markets, what are base-building markets? How do you know that the long position, not protected by a stop loss order, will not collapse if the market breaks away to the downside? If you are trading stocks, there is some sort of intrinsic value the market doesn't trade under. For example, how much lower can a $2 stock go?

Unfortunately, value in the futures market is not based on something as abstract as earnings and sales, but rather on utility value. In the two commodities of corn and wheat, wheat prices historically trade above the price of corn. If the supply of wheat is great the price will go down below the price of corn until the wheat can be used as feed for livestock, at which price it should stop going down. That's the utility value. If corn prices, however, go lower than the wheat, so will wheat prices. What does a trader do in cases like these where there is a limitless bottom to the price of wheat? This has occurred infrequently, probably no more than four or five times in the history of recorded prices from the Chicago Board of Trade.

Now you can understand the problem with trying to being so precise about applying rules to the markets based on other preexisting conditions. It makes more sense, and is more practical, to just slap on the positions and place the stop loss order far enough that it won't get caught in a normal reaction. Why bother to think about the market condition of your order? It is important to know whether or not you're in a breakout stage or in a runaway market, but by indiscriminately placing stop loss orders you will absolutely protect your equity whether your analysis is correct or not and ultimately, whether or not you have gauged the current market condition to be either trending or trading. Until your skills in assessing market conditions improve, you must use stops. Even after you've developed such assessment skills, you should still use stops!

"Use stops indiscriminately" might be the wrong phrase to use here, but it highlights my point that you must use safeguards, regardless of how inane, in the markets.

To trade otherwise is to add to the complexity of the analysis, something to which a trader like myself is averse.

RULE 49

Ignore Statistical
Reports in Bear Markets

Play bear markets differently than bull markets when
it comes to using statistical reports. It is generally
accepted practice to disregard statistical reports on securities together with records of past earnings and dividends.

My self-training and experience has taught me that
in bear markets, sell anything and everything. First sell
out all longs, then sell short. Are there any exceptions,
i.e., going long in bear markets? Yes, but to find the
exceptions is similar to trying to find the proverbial needle in a haystack: it's possible, but not probable. Don't
waste your efforts to find the needle; your time can be
efficiently used to find the next weak stock to short. It
will be lining up for you to pick out.

In the same manner that all stocks go up in a bull
market, all stocks go down in a bear market. You will be
exposing yourself to guaranteed losses by going long in
bear markets.

If the public was enchanted with a stock during the late stages of the bull market cycle, you can expect the stock to drop more when the public becomes disenchanted with the stock's performance in the bear market. It's in the nature of market action. The heros of yesterday's bull market will be among the first to be rounded up and shot in the next bear market.

How do statistics and fundamentals enter into the analysis of these stocks? Very simply: they will turn out bad, again supporting reasons why the stocks must be sold or shorted.

The degree of bearishness of the markets can be inferred if a group of stocks in the same industry drops when bullish news appears for one of its members; the degrees of bearishness diminish from the weakest to the strongest stock in that industry, which is only logical. If you are a portfolio manager interested in personal computer stocks and all have been taking hits to the downside because of the general bearishness of the markets you will be looking for reasons to liquidate your holdings in the personal computer industry. If a bullish set of numbers comes out for one still bullish stock in that group, you will unload your other stocks in that group and concentrate your buying in that one bullish stock— pure Darwinism in action. The strong get stronger and the weak get weaker.

At best, the future numbers for most sectors will show weakness. You must get rid of all longs in bear markets because of fundamental reasons; these numbers will worsen as the bear market ensues. You must go short in bear markets because of timing techniques. Understand the distinction between ridding yourself of longs and going short; understand the use of fundamental numbers and technical techniques.

You must ignore all statistical numbers in bear markets and concentrate on market action instead because the numbers which are coming out at the present are

reflective of what happened, not what will be happening.
In general all these statistical numbers reflect generally
better numbers from the past than what will be shown
later, which are results of the present and the immediate future.

In bear markets you don't have the same privileges
that come with bull markets. In bull markets, you can
delay your entry into a stock that is going up in price.
You don't lose money, but you lose potential profits by
getting involved in this lead of price versus lag of statistical numbers. In bear markets, you actually lose money
if you buy because prices erode while you are holding
the positions. By the time the real reasons come out, you
will have lost substantial amounts of money.

The correct way to play bear markets is to sell in
anticipation of weaker statistical numbers.

What good does it do you if last quarter's earnings
were unchanged from the previous quarter's when the
price action of the stock is reflecting bearishness by
going down? By the time you get the numbers to justify
the price action this quarter, the price will have eroded
further! Yes, you will eventually get the numbers which
will justify the current pricing, but by then the pricing
would have dropped as much as it could already. You
will then be sitting with a large unrealized loss in your
holdings.

Round numbers for stocks such as $50, $75, $100,
etc., were markers in the past for these stocks on the
way up. These same price levels will not hold as support
and reversal areas in bear markets. On the way up they
were areas of buying; on the way down they will be price
areas of supply. Over the last several years I've noticed a
perverse interest on the part of traders to purposefully
try to push prices immediately past these numbers in
either direction. It's sort of a challenge to them to see if
they can crack these even numbers. In the past there
were temporary reversals. Nowadays, I don't know

276

whether or not the types of players in the markets are more sophisticated, but these levels appear as challenges to traders. These traders are intent on pushing past these even numbers, some even on the first try.

RULE 50

Don't Forget What Procedures Were Designed For

As the son of immigrant parents who once owned a restaurant business I have a story to relate to you that will illustrate this rule clearly.

My parents have been in the restaurant business for years. Shortly after they opened their restaurant several thugs robbed them. In they walked one summer evening and demanded money from my parents. Out they ran afterward with the day's receipts.

My parents became wary of being robbed again. So they guarded against it and were never robbed again. Face to face, at least.

Instead several times the thugs chose to break into the business at night after all the employees had left. Each time they ransacked the business and took money from the register and the safe.

So, my parents took the end of day receipts and started hiding them in the refrigerator. After several more break-ins the thugs could find no money in the register or the safe, and they decided to leave my parents' restaurant alone.

About a year later my mother shrieked for joy from the dining room and rushed over to me. She said she found some money under one of the booths. It was one day's receipts from several months earlier. She considered it found money.

Puzzled, I asked her why they had left money under the booth. She said that since the break-ins they had varied the location of the hiding place of the end of day receipts.

It sounded okay to me at the time they told me this. However, the more I thought about it, the sillier it got.

Apparently my parents had hidden the receipts every night, first in only one place and then in many different places. Their pattern of hiding the money evolved into a warped strategy. It got to the point that since a second hiding place evoked no theft, then a third hiding place should do the same, and so forth.

One night they hid the money in the refrigerator, another night the storage room, yet another night the microwave oven. They had done this for a year and in the process they increased their chances of losing track of where they hid some of the money. That's why they were overjoyed to have "found" the money again in a hiding place. In the end instead of hiding the money from would-be criminals they had hidden the money from themselves. The thefts caused them to be overwhelmed to the point that their actions were illogical but served to suppress their anxieties. The thieves came in once, but this small component part of their lives evolved into affecting a larger portion of their lives.

We often do this in our own lives. In the process of trying to find solutions to our trading problems we are forever looking for solutions which don't resolve the problems, but suppress the immediate anxieties. Unlike my parents' approach, your systematic approach to trading success in the markets mustn't be so set in stone that you lose sight of what it is you are trying to accomplish. The solutions to your trading problems can be found right on your doorsteps, if only you stop to look at what you are trying to achieve in trading or investing.

I'm also urging you to create a methodology for trading and then reinforce that method for as long as you can, instead of flitting around, to and fro, from system to system, from methodology to methodology.

The answers to all your trading problems, believe it or not, really can be found within yourself.

Once I told my parents that one single location for hiding their money at night would resolve the problem of losing track of the many places they found in the large restaurant, they never lost that money again! You get it, dear readers? They never lost that money again!

The more complex the problem, the simpler the solution.

INDEX

INDEX

INDEX